walkermaths 1.13

ELEMENTS OF CHANCE

NCEA Level 1 Internal

Charlotte Walker and Victoria Walker

Walker Maths 1.13 Elements of Chance
1st Edition
Charlotte Walker
Victoria Walker

Designer: Cheryl Smith, Macarn Design
Production controller: Siew Han Ong

Any URLs contained in this publication were checked for currency during the production process. Note, however, that the publisher cannot vouch for the ongoing currency of URLs.

Acknowledgements
Cover photo courtesy of Shutterstock.

We wish to thank the Boards of Trustees of Darfield and Riccarton High Schools for allowing us to use materials and ideas developed while teaching. Our thanks also go to all past and present colleagues, especially Kath Wilson, who have generously shared their experience and ideas.

For product information and technology assistance,
in Australia call **1300 790 853**;
in New Zealand call **0800 449 725**

For permission to use material from this text or product, please email **aust.permissions@cengage.com**

National Library of New Zealand Cataloguing-in-Publication Data
A catalogue record for this book is available from the National Library of New Zealand.

978 0 17041602 3

Cengage Learning Australia
Level 7, 80 Dorcas Street
South Melbourne, Victoria Australia 3205

Cengage Learning New Zealand
Unit 4B Rosedale Office Park
331 Rosedale Road, Albany, North Shore 0632, NZ

For learning solutions, visit **cengage.co.nz**

Printed in China by 1010 Printing International Limited
4 5 6 7 23 22

CONTENTS

ISBN: 9780170416023

Glossary

Make your own glossary of key terms:

Term	Definition	Picture/Example
Probability		
Frequency		
Proportion		
Percentage		
Experiment		
Experimental probability		
Theoretical probability		
Trial		
Outcome		
Event		
Either		
A fair die		

ISBN: 9780170416023

Statistical enquiry cycle

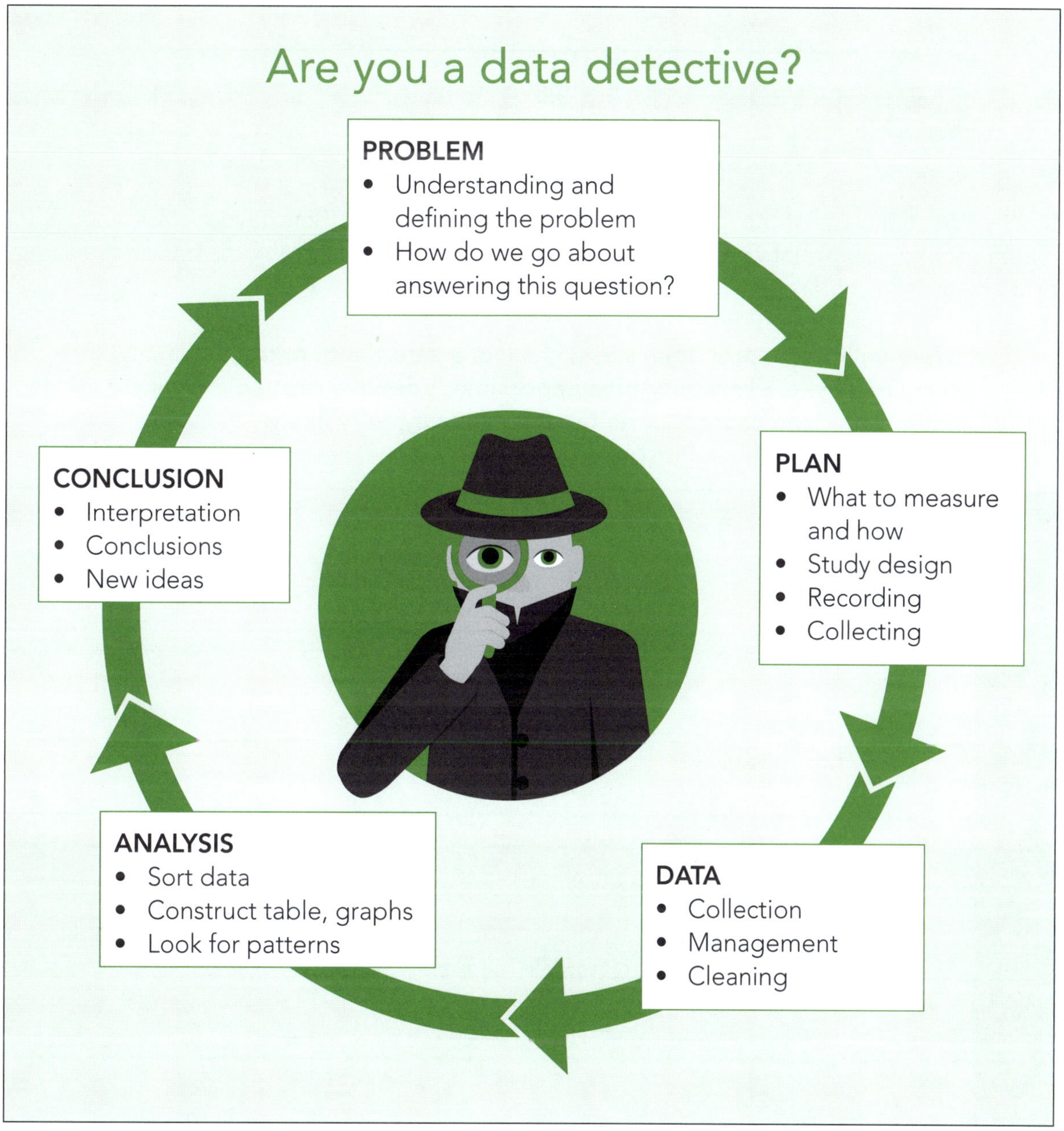

Are you a data detective?

PROBLEM
- Understanding and defining the problem
- How do we go about answering this question?

PLAN
- What to measure and how
- Study design
- Recording
- Collecting

DATA
- Collection
- Management
- Cleaning

ANALYSIS
- Sort data
- Construct table, graphs
- Look for patterns

CONCLUSION
- Interpretation
- Conclusions
- New ideas

Probability

The range of values for probabilities

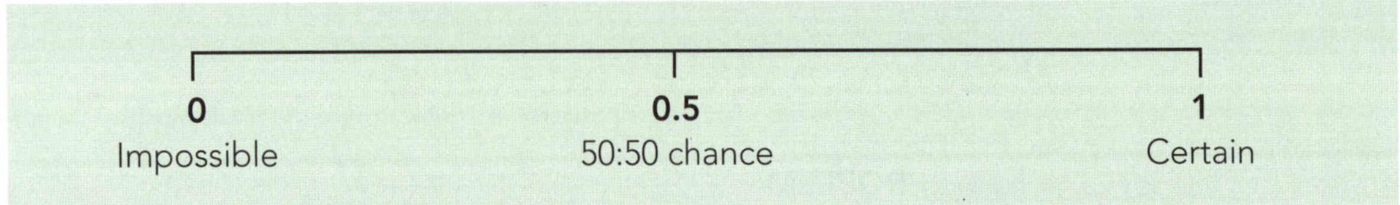

Discuss the meanings of the following words and phrases with others in your class, and match each to appropriate probability value(s). You may have several words beside the same probability value, and some words can cover several probability values.

Very unlikely, improbable, slight chance, a sure thing, extremely likely, certain, maybe, likely, fifty-fifty, impossible, possible, probable, unlikely, no chance, definite, even, no way, very likely.

0	
0.1	
0.2	
0.3	
0.4	
0.5	
0.6	
0.7	
0.8	
0.9	
1.0	

ISBN: 9780170416023

Using numbers for writing probabilities

- Probabilities can be written as fractions, decimals or percentages.
- You can convert between these with your calculator.
- When you want to compare probabilities, you should always use decimals.

Example: Write the probability $\frac{7}{16}$ as a decimal. 7 [÷] 16 [=] 0.4375

Convert the following probabilities to decimals, and state which of each pair is more likely.

1 $\frac{7}{16}$ = ________ $\frac{1}{3}$ = ________

Most likely: ____________________

2 $\frac{3}{4}$ = ________ $\frac{8}{11}$ = ________

Most likely: ____________________

3 $\frac{17}{18}$ = ________ $\frac{19}{20}$ = ________

Most likely: ____________________

4 $\frac{13}{24}$ = ________ $\frac{27}{50}$ = ________

Most likely: ____________________

5 $\frac{11}{20}$ = ________ $\frac{7}{13}$ = ________

Most likely: ____________________

6 $\frac{6}{17}$ = ________ $\frac{3}{8}$ = ________

Most likely: ____________________

Test yourself

For the following sentences, indicate whether each statement could be correct or is impossible. Justify your decision.

1 Hunter says that the probability of winning at Jenga when he plays his best friend is $\frac{1}{20}$.

____

2 When Millie plays paper, scissors, rock with her two friends, she thinks she can win half the time.

____

3 When Harry plays his friend at Scrabble, he thinks he wins 110% of the games.

____

4 Jessie says that the probability that she will win Lotto is –0.1.

____

ISBN: 9780170416023

Ways of calculating probabilities

1 Equally likely outcomes

- This is where every possible outcome is equally likely to occur.
- An example is throwing a fair die: you are equally likely to get a 1, 2, 3, 4, 5 or 6.

$$\textbf{Probability} = \frac{\textbf{number of favourable outcomes}}{\textbf{total possible outcomes}}$$

With a single event

Example 1: For a fair die:

$P(6) = \frac{1}{6}$ or $0.1\dot{6}$

$P(1 \text{ or } 2) = \frac{2}{6}$ or $\frac{1}{3}$ or $0.\dot{3}$

Example 2: For the spinner shown in the diagram:

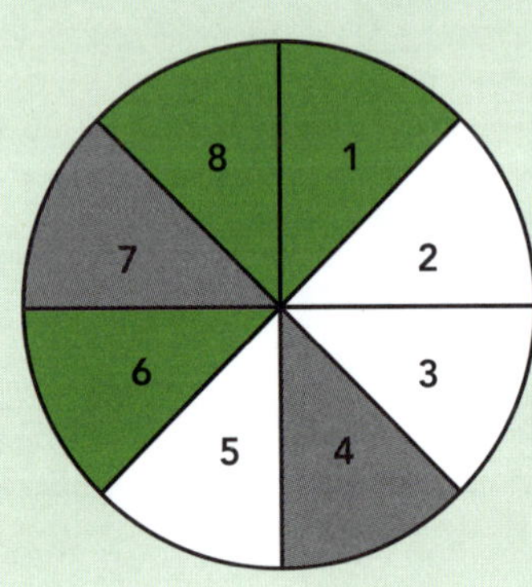

$P(7) = \frac{1}{8}$ or 0.125

$P(\text{grey}) = P(4 \text{ or } 7) = \frac{2}{8}$ or 0.25

Notice that 1 is both green and odd, but we include it just **once** in the list.

$P(\text{green or odd number}) = P(1, 6, 8, 3, 5 \text{ or } 7) = \frac{6}{8}$ or 0.75

$P(\text{white and odd}) = P(3 \text{ or } 5) = \frac{2}{8}$ or 0.25

$P(\text{green and } 7) = \frac{0}{8}$ or 0

Calculate the following probabilities.
When tossing a fair die:

1 P(3) = ____________________

2 P(4, 5 or 6) = ____________________

3 P(odd number) = P(____________________) = ____________________

4 P(not a 6) = P(____________________) = ____________________

5 P(5 or an even number) = P(____________________) = ____________________

6 P(7) = ____________________

7 P(1, 2, 3, 4, 5 or 6) = ____________________

ISBN: 9780170416023

Anna created a different spinner:

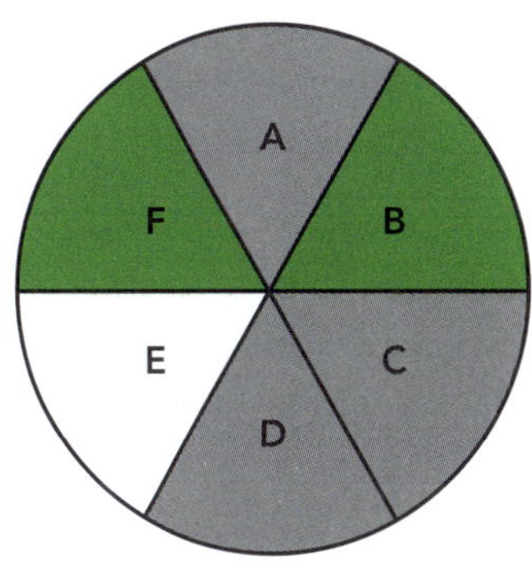

8 P(F) = ________

9 P(A or B) = ________

10 P(grey) = P(________) = ________

11 P(not grey) = P(________) = ________

12 P(G) = ________

13 P(grey or letter in the word 'bed') = P(________) = ________

14 P(grey and letter in the word 'bed') = P(________) = ________

Mike has a bag of lollies which are the same apart from their colour. It contains 7 red lollies, 3 green ones, 5 yellow ones and 9 white ones. He puts his hand in the bag and selects a lolly at random. After he has looked at it, he puts it back in the bag.

15 P(red) = ________

16 P(not getting a red) = ________

17 P(red or green) = ________

18 P(not getting a red or green) = ________

19 P(white, red or green) = ________

20 P(not yellow) = ________

21 P(black) = ________

22 P(red, green, yellow or white) = ________

Fetu has a set of dominoes. Each domino has two halves, with between 0 and 6 spots at each end. There are 28 dominoes in a full set. He places all his dominoes upside down on the floor, and turns one over at random. After he has looked at it, he turns it over and mixes the dominoes up.

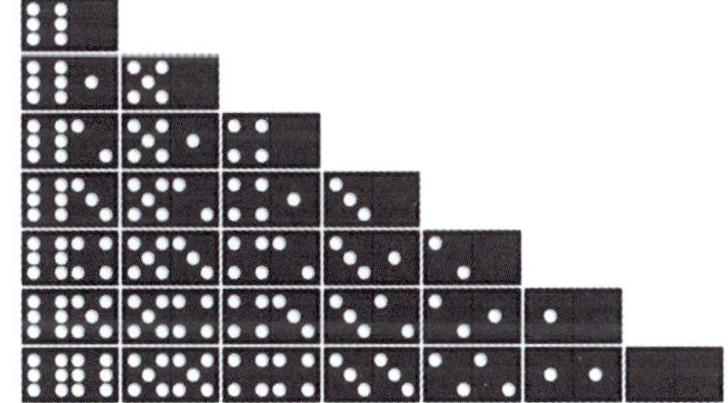

23 P(a domino with no dots on it) = ________

24 P(a domino with the same number of dots at each end) = ________

25 P(a domino with five at one end and three at the other end) = ________

26 P(a domino which has exactly one five on it) = ________

27 P(a domino with a total of four dots on it) = ________

ISBN: 9780170416023

Combining two events

- It is useful to use equally likely outcomes where **two** actions are performed, such as tossing a coin and throwing a die.
- It usually makes calculations easier if you create a **table** showing all the possible outcomes.

Nikau tosses a coin and throws a die. The table shows the possible outcomes:

	1	2	3	4	5	6
H	H 1	H 2	H 3	H 4	H 5	H 6
T	T 1	T 2	T 3	T 4	T 5	T 6

There are 12 different outcomes.

P(H) = $\frac{6}{12}$ or 0.5

P(3) = $\frac{2}{12}$ or $0.1\dot{6}$

P(H and a 3) = $\frac{1}{12}$ or $0.08\dot{3}$

P(H or a 3) = $\frac{7}{12}$ or $0.58\dot{3}$

Frank is playing a board game in which two dice are tossed at the same time. One is **black** and the other is **green**. The possible outcomes can be shown in the table below:

	1	2	3	4	5	6
1	1 1	1 2				
2	2 1	2 2				
3						
4						
5						
6						

1 Complete the table.

2 How many different possible outcomes are there? ____________________

3 List the outcomes that add to 3: ____________________

4 P(total is 3) = ____________

5 P(total is 5) = ____________

6 P(total is 3 or 5) = ____________

7 P(total is more than 10) = ____________

8 P(total is 10 or less) = ____________

9 P(total is even) = ____________

10 P(two numbers the same) = ____________

11 P(green die is more than black die) = ____________

 ISBN: 9780170416023

In another game, Frank uses a spinner with the numbers 1, 2, 4 and 8, and he tosses a die.

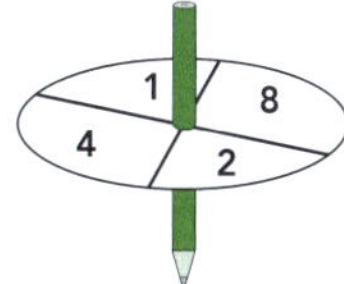

12 Complete the table to show all the possible outcomes.

	1					6
1		1 2				
	2 1			2 4		
			4 3			
8						8 6

13 P(total is 2) = ____________

14 P(two numbers the same) = ____________

15 P(odd total) = ____________

16 P(total is more than 10) = ____________

Aria has a coin and a tetrahedral die (four equal faces). The die has the numbers 1, 2, 3 or 4 on each face.

17 Use the space below to draw a table of the possible outcomes when she tosses the coin and throws the die.

18 P(H and 1) = ____________

19 P(H) = ____________

20 P(H and 6) = ____________

21 P(T or 3) = ____________

ISBN: 9780170416023

2 Long run probability

- Sometimes the probability of an event is **difficult or impossible** to calculate.
- In these cases we do **many trials** and record the number of times an event occurs.
- Often the true value of the probability will **never** be known.
- **The greater the number of trials, the closer our estimate for the probability will be to the true probability.**

$$\textbf{Probability} = \frac{\textbf{number of times an event occurs}}{\textbf{total number of trials}}$$

Example: Hugo kept a record of how he travelled to school last year. He went to school on 178 days. He biked on 102 days, walked on 24 days, and caught the bus on the other days. Calculate the probabilities that he biked, walked and caught the bus.

P(Hugo **bikes** to school) $= \dfrac{\text{number of times he has biked to school in the last year}}{\text{total number of school days in the last year}}$

$= \dfrac{102}{178} = 0.5730$

P(Hugo **walks** to school) $= \dfrac{\text{number of times he has walked to school in the last year}}{\text{total number of school days in the last year}}$

$= \dfrac{24}{178} = 0.1348$

P(Hugo **buses** to school) $= \dfrac{\text{number of times he has bused to school in the last year}}{\text{total number of school days in the last year}}$

$= \dfrac{52}{178} = 0.2921$

Answer the following questions.

1 Marama was in the same class as Hugo, and she also kept records of how she got to school. She went to school on 180 days. She caught the bus on 126 days. She walked on 41 days. Her mum drove her on the remaining days.
Calculate the probabilities that she caught the bus, walked and was driven.

____

____

____

2 There are 28 students in their class. In their probability test, 7 students got Excellence grades, 13 got Merit, 6 got Achieved, and 2 got Not Achieved. Calculate the probabilities of getting each grade.

____

____

____

ISBN: 9780170416023

3 A survey of the number of pets owned by the families of 160 secondary school students produced the following results:

Number of pets	Number of students
0	36
1	59
2	29
3	15
More than 3	21

a What is the probability that a student's family owns no pets?

____

b What is the probability that a student's family owns one or two pets?

____

c What percentage of students' families owned more than one pet?

____

Reminder: percentage = probability x 100%
e.g. probability = 0.27
⇒ percentage = 0.27 x 100% = 27%

4 The same survey asked students about their lunches on school days.

Source of lunch	Number of students
Had no lunch	13
Packed lunch from home	74
Bought on the way to school	25
Bought from canteen	48

a What is the probability that a student has no lunch?

____

b What is the probability that a student bought their lunch?

____

c What percentage of students eat lunch?

____

5 The same survey asked students how they had got to school that morning.

How they got to school	Number of students
Walked	
Skateboard	17
On a bus	52
Motor bike or motor scooter	9
By car — drove themselves	16
By car — driven by somebody else	27

a How many students walked to school?

____

b What is the probability that a student came to school on a bus?

____

c What is the probability that a student came to school by motorised transport?

____

ISBN: 9780170416023

Expected number of outcomes

Expected number of outcomes = P(event) x number of trials

Example 1: Amy tosses a die 120 times. How many times can she expect a 6?

Expected number of 6s $= P(6) \times 120$

$= 0.1\dot{6} \times 120$

$= 20$

Example 2: The probability of a person being struck by lightning in the USA is $\frac{1}{700\,000}$ in one year. If in 2015 the population of the USA was 322 584 000, calculate the expected number of people who were struck by lightning during 2015.

Expected number of people struck by lightning $= \frac{1}{700\,000} \times 322\,584\,000$

$= 461$

The exact answer is 460.83…., but this is people, so we must round to the nearest whole person.

Answer the following questions.

1 Archie flips a coin 80 times and records the results. How many 'heads' can he expect?

2 Nick tossed a die 90 times and recorded the results. How many times can he expect to get a 5 or a 6?

3 The probability of being left-handed is 0.1. If your school roll is 793, how many people would you expect to be left-handed at your school?

4 The probability of boys being colour-blind is 0.08. If there are 32 colour blind boys at your school, how many boys attend your school?

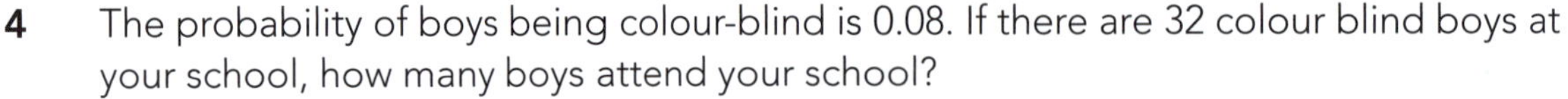

5 The probability of an egg having two yolks is 0.001. If a farm produces 150 dozen eggs each week, how many would you expect to have two yolks?

6 In the game of poker, each player is dealt a hand of five cards. A full house is when a hand contains three of a kind and a pair, for example K, K, K, Q, Q. The probability that a hand contains a full house is 0.1441. If 72 hands are dealt during the course of a game, how many of these would be expected to contain a full house?

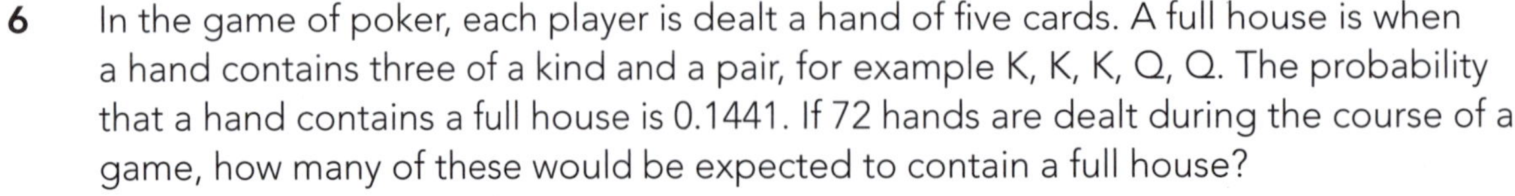

ISBN: 9780170416023

Combining probabilities — probability trees

Probability trees are very useful for calculating probabilities where several events occur.

Example: Arthur had a bag of lollies. It contained 7 yellow ones and 3 red ones. Without looking, he selected a lolly and ate it. Then he selected a second lolly and ate it.

a What is the probability that he ate two yellow ones?

b What is the probability that he ate one of each colour?

Steps:

1 Decide what the **events** are, and their order:

Event 1 will be the colour of the first lolly.
Event 2 will be the colour of the second lolly.

Write the **events** at the **ends** of the branches:

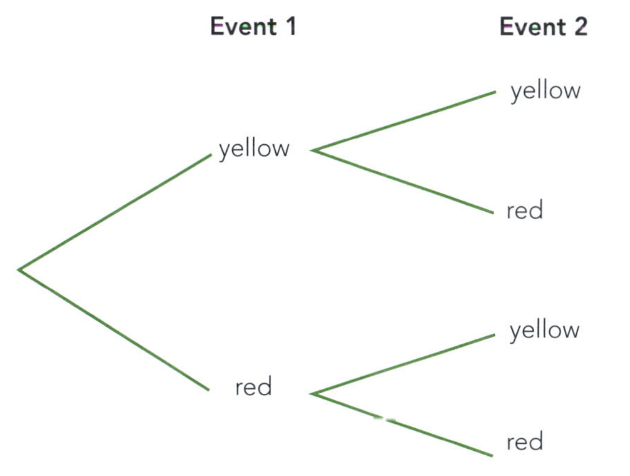

2 Add the **probabilities** of each event to the **middle** of each branch:

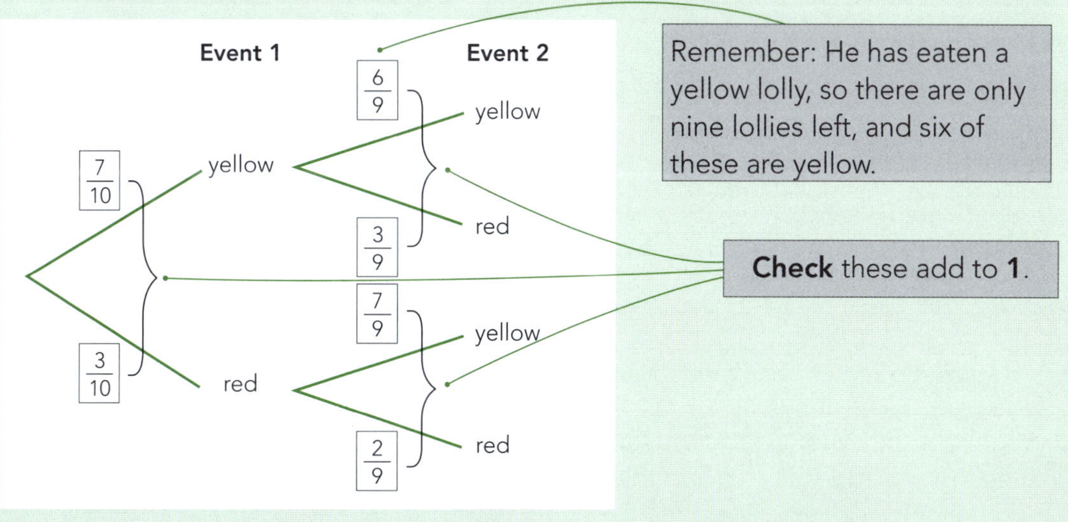

3 **Check** that the probabilities for every pair of branches adds to **1**.

ISBN: 9780170416023

4 **List** the outcomes at the ends of each branch, and calculate the probabilities at each end. You **multiply** the probabilities along each branch because Event 1 **and** Event 2 must occur.

It is often easiest to keep probabilities as fractions with the same denominator.

Event 1 | **Event 2**

$\frac{7}{10}$ yellow — $\frac{6}{9}$ yellow: $P(\mathbf{yy}) = \frac{7}{10} \times \frac{6}{9} = \frac{42}{90} = 0.4\dot{6}$ } **a**

$\frac{7}{10}$ yellow — $\frac{3}{9}$ red: $P(\mathbf{yr}) = \frac{7}{10} \times \frac{3}{9} = \frac{21}{90} = 0.2\dot{3}$

$\frac{3}{10}$ red — $\frac{7}{9}$ yellow: $P(\mathbf{ry}) = \frac{3}{10} \times \frac{7}{9} = \frac{21}{90} = 0.2\dot{3}$ } **b**

$\frac{3}{10}$ red — $\frac{2}{9}$ red: $P(\mathbf{rr}) = \frac{3}{10} \times \frac{2}{9} = \frac{6}{90} = 0.0\dot{6}$

$\frac{90}{90} = 1.00$

Check these add to **1**.

5 **Check** that your probabilities in the right-hand column **add** to **1**. This is because **one** of these options **must** occur.

Useful tips:

1 **Addition Rule:** if one event **OR** another happens $\Rightarrow$ **ADD** the probabilities.

2 **Multiplication Rule:** if one event **AND** another happens $\Rightarrow$ **MULTIPLY** the probabilities.

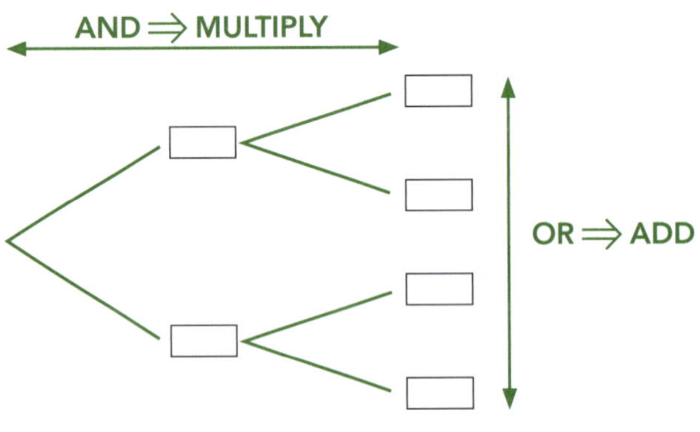

6 Highlight the event(s) required, along with their probabilities. If necessary, **add** these to find the overall probability required.

a What is the probability that he ate two yellow ones? $P(yy) = 0.4\dot{6}$

b What is the probability that he ate one of each colour? $P(yr \text{ or } ry) = 0.2\dot{3} + 0.2\dot{3} = 0.4\dot{6}$

ISBN: 9780170416023

Use probability trees to answer the following questions.

1 Angus had a bag of lollies. He had 5 orange ones and 3 green ones. Without looking, he selected a lolly and then put it back in the bag. He selected and ate a second lolly.

a Complete the probability tree.

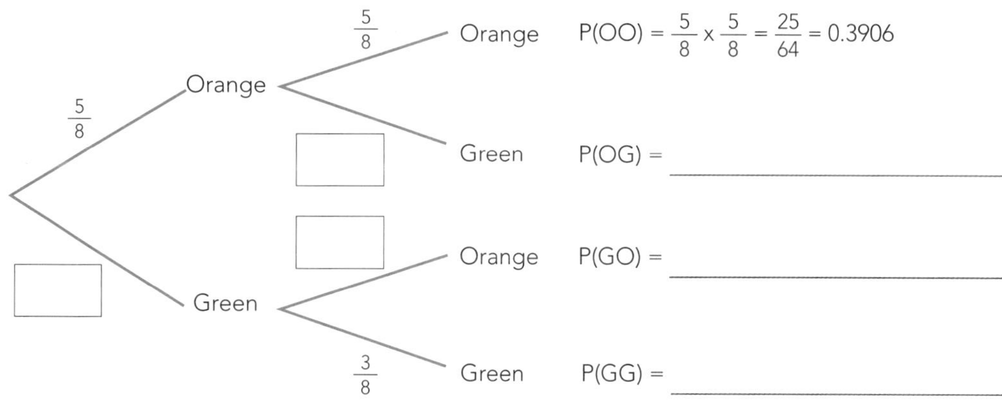

b What is the probability that he selected two orange lollies?

c What is the probability that he selected one of each colour?

d What is the probability that he selected two of the same colour?

e What is the probability that he doesn't select an orange lolly?

f What is the probability that he selects at least one green lolly?

g If he repeated the experiment 200 times (without eating any), how many times could he expect to get two orange lollies?

h If he repeated the experiment 200 times (without eating any), how many times could he expect to get at least one green lolly?

ISBN: 9780170416023

2 Matiu had a bag of lollies. He had 5 pink ones and 3 blue ones. Without looking, he selected a lolly and ate it. He selected a second lolly and ate that as well.

a Complete the probability tree.

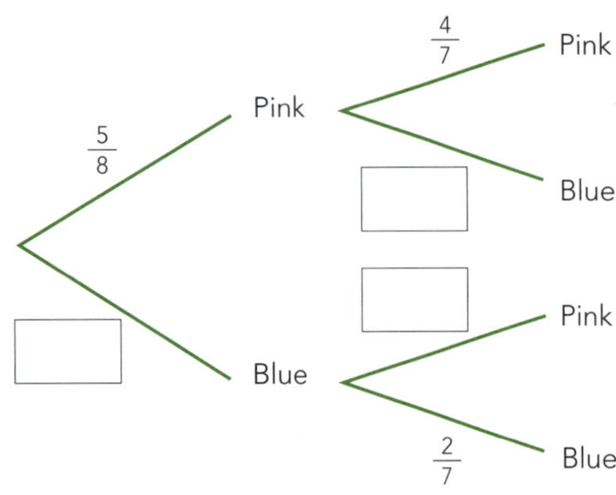

$P(PP) = \frac{5}{8} \times \frac{4}{7} = \frac{20}{56} = 0.3571$

P(PB) = ______________________

P(BP) = ______________________

P(BB) = ______________________

b What is the probability that he ate two pink ones?

____

c What is the probability that he ate one of each colour?

____

d What is the probability that he ate two of the same colour?

____

e What is the probability that he doesn't eat a pink lolly?

____

f What is the probability that he gets at least one blue lolly?

____

g If he repeated this experiment 200 times (without eating any), how many times could he expect to get two pink lollies?

____

h If he repeated this experiment 200 times (without eating any), how many times could he expect to get at least one blue lolly?

____

ISBN: 9780170416023

3 Amber tossed a coin and then threw a four-sided die. Three sides of the die have a spot and the fourth side has a plus sign.

a Complete the probability tree.

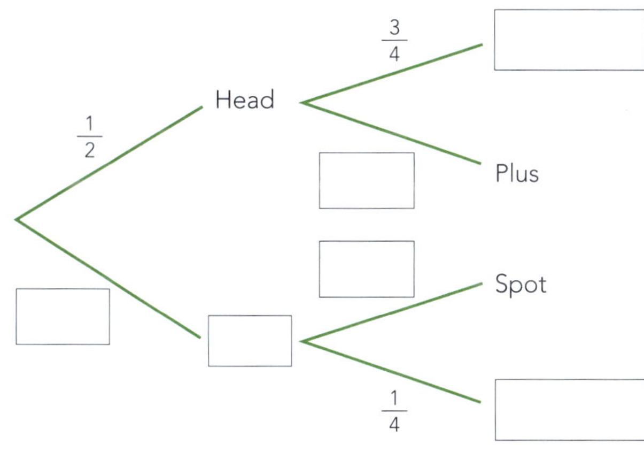

$P(HS) = \frac{1}{2} \times \frac{3}{4} = \frac{3}{8} = 0.375$

P(HP) = ______________________

P(TS) = ______________________

P(TP) = ______________________

b What is the probability that she gets a head?

____

c What is the probability that she gets a tail and a plus?

____

d What is the probability that she gets a tail and a spot?

____

e What is the probability that she gets either a head or a spot?

____

f What is the probability that she gets either a tail or a plus?

____

g What is the probability that she gets neither a tail nor a plus?

____

h What is the probability that she gets neither a tail nor a spot?

____

ISBN: 9780170416023

4 Sometimes when people play Snakes and Ladders they use the rule that nobody can start the game until they have thrown a 6. The probability tree below shows the possible outcomes for the first two throws of the die.

a Complete the probability tree.

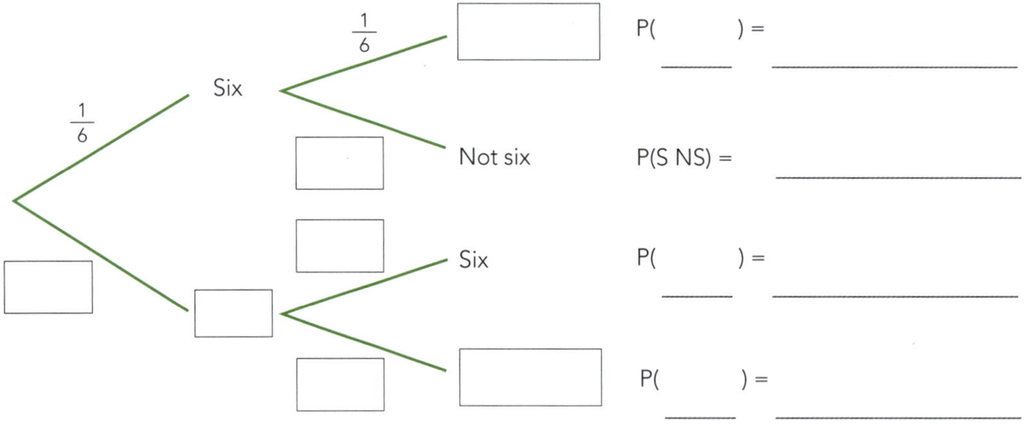

b What is the probability that a player gets a 6 on the first throw?

c What is the probability that a player gets a 'not 6' and then a 6?

d What is the probability that a player gets a 6 in the first two throws?

e What is the probability that a player doesn't get a 6 in the first two throws?

f What do you notice about your last two answers. Why?

g If Thomas recorded the dice throws for the starts of 80 games of Snakes and Ladders, how many would be expected to result in a start within the first two throws?

h What is the probability that a player gets to start on the third throw?

  ISBN: 9780170416023

5 Georgia devises a game for the school fair. Players contribute a $1 coin and a $2 coin, which they toss. The rules are:

tossing two heads ⇒ their $3 is returned, plus an additional $3
tossing one head ⇒ they get just their $1 coin back
tossing no heads ⇒ they get nothing back.

Sketch your own probability tree for this situation.

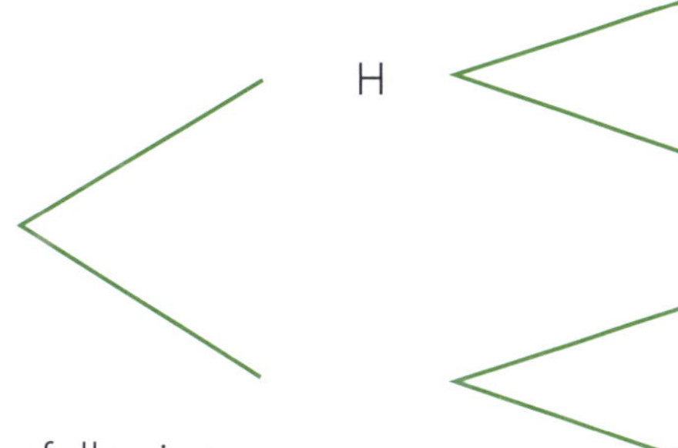

Use it to calculate the following.

a The probability that the $3 is returned, plus an additional $3. ____________

b The probability that a player gets back their $1 coin only. ____________

c The percentage of players who get back $1 or less. ____________

d If she repeated this 100 times, how many times would she expect to get no heads?

____

6 A recent survey showed that 80% of students use Facebook and 30% use Twitter. Sketch your own probability tree for this situation.

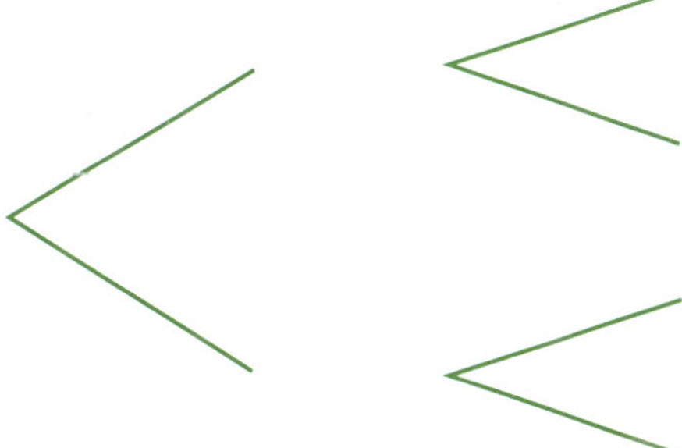

Use it to calculate the following.

a The probability that a student uses both Facebook and Twitter. ____________

b The percentage of students who use just one of these services. ____________

c In a school with 822 students, how many would be expected to use Twitter?

____

d In the same school, how many would be expected to use neither service?

____

ISBN: 9780170416023

Mixing it up

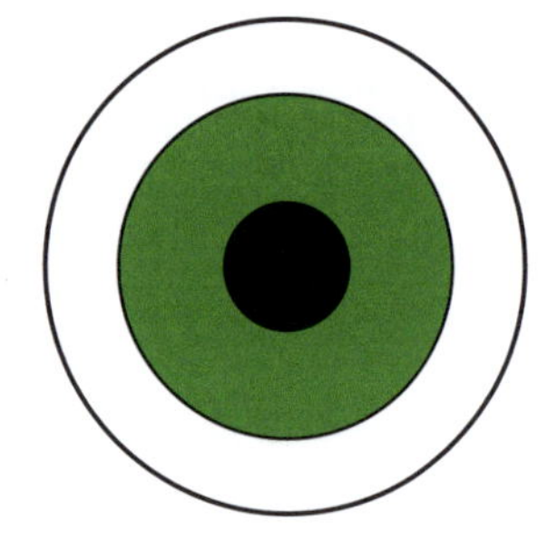

1 Zoe created a simple dartboard. She calculated that if a dart landed on the dartboard:

- the probability of a dart hitting the black was $\frac{1}{8}$
- the probability of a dart hitting the green was $\frac{3}{8}$, and
- the probability of a dart hitting the white was $\frac{1}{2}$.

Assuming that a dart hit the dartboard, calculate the following probabilities.

a P(dart hit the black, green or white) = ______________________

b P(dart did not hit the green) = ______________________

c P(dart hit the green or white) = ______________________

d If she threw 80 darts that all hit the dartboard, how many should she expect to land in the green or the white? ____

Zoe threw two darts at the dartboard, and both hit it. Calculate the following probabilities.

e P(both darts hit the white) = ______________________

f P(neither dart hits the white) = ______________________

g If neither lands in the white, then the probability a dart lands on the black becomes $\frac{1}{4}$ and the probability that a dart lands on the green becomes $\frac{3}{4}$.
Draw a probability tree to show the possible outcomes for these two darts.

i P(first dart hit the black and second dart hit the green) = ___________________

ii P(a dart hit the black and the other hit the green) = ______________________

iii If she threw 80 **pairs** of darts that all hit the dartboard, for how many of the pairs should she expect both to land in the green?

____

 ISBN: 9780170416023

2 Jean is playing a game of Snakes and Ladders and she is on square 96. These are the rules for the end of the game:

- When it is your turn, you throw a die and move forward the number of squares shown.
- If you land on the tail of the snake (e.g. square 97), you will slide down to square 65.
- To win you must land exactly on square 100. You may not overshoot.
- If you throw a number which will make you overshoot, you do not move during that turn.

The only way to win the game in **one** move is to throw a **4**.
She can win the game in **two** moves by throwing any one of the following in the order shown:

(6, 4), (5, 4), (2, 2) or (3, 1).

Calculate the following probabilities.

a P(she wins in one turn) = ______________________

b P(she wins in exactly two turns) = ______________________

The table shows the probability distribution for Jean finishing the game in one, two or more than two turns.

Turns to finish	one	two	more than two
Probability			

c Add your answers from **a** and **b** to the table, and use them to help you calculate the probability that she wins in more than two turns.

d She performed an experiment in which she did 60 trials starting from square 96. She found that it took more than two moves for her to finish in 39 of these trials. Using her data from the experiment, calculate the probability that she finished in more than two moves:

P(finished in more than two moves) = ______________________

e Compare this probability with your answer from **c**. Does it seem reasonable?

____

____

____

f What would you expect if she had done 200 trials?

____

____

ISBN: 9780170416023

Probability investigations

1 Planning an investigation

You need to:
- Pose an appropriate **question**, or make a **statement** about a situation involving probability.
- List all the possible **outcomes**. These must relate to the question.
- State the **event** you are interested in.
- **Describe** how you will carry out your investigation.
- State the **number** of **trials** you will perform, or the **number** of **observations** you will make.
- Make a **prediction**.

a Questions, trials, outcomes and events

- You will be **given a general context** as the basis for your probability investigation.
- You need to think of a **question** that can be answered by performing a **probability experiment** within this context.
- A **trial** is one performance of your experiment.
- The **outcomes** of an experiment are all the possible results, with respect to the question, from one trial.
- An **event** is the outcome from a trial which is of interest in your question.

Examples:

1 Throwing five dice at once.

Question	One trial	Outcomes	Event
If I roll five dice together, what is the probability that I will get fewer than two sixes?	*One roll of five dice together.*	• *Getting 0 or 1 six.* • *Getting 2, 3, 4 or 5 sixes.*	• *Getting 0 or 1 six.*

Make sure that every possibility is covered by your two outcomes. In this case you **must** throw 0, 1, 2, 3, 4 or 5 sixes.

2 Kicking a rugby ball.

Question	One trial	Outcomes	Event
Harry has four rugby balls, and he tries to kick goals from the 22-metre line. He would like to know the probability that he gets three or four goals from each group of four attempts.	*Having four tries to kick a goal.*	• *Kicking 0, 1 or 2 goals.* • *Kicking 3 or 4 goals.*	• *Kicking 3 or 4 goals.*

ISBN: 9780170416023

Complete the table. Later in the book you will complete investigations for **Questions 1** and **2**.

Question	One trial	Outcomes	Event
Question 1 If I roll two dice and add their numbers, what is the probability that they add to 10 or more?	____________ ____________ ____________	• Getting dice that add to 2, 3, 4, 5, 6, 7, 8 or 9. • ____________ ____________	• ____________ ____________
Question 2 If I have five shots at getting a netball through the hoop from just inside the circle, what is the probability that I get fewer than three through the hoop?	____________ ____________ ____________	• ____________ ____________ • ____________ ____________	• ____________ ____________
I have a bag containing 10 lollies: 4 red, 3 green, 2 yellow and 1 blue. If I pick two lollies together, what is the probability that they are different colours?	____________ ____________ ____________	• ____________ ____________ • ____________ ____________	• ____________ ____________
I have a bag containing 10 lollies: 4 red, 3 green, 2 yellow and 1 blue. If I pick lollies one at a time without replacement, ____________ ____________	____________ ____________ ____________	• ____________ ____________ • ____________ ____________	• Picking 4 or more lollies before getting a red one.
When tossing a coin three times, ____________ ____________	____________ ____________ ____________	• ____________ ____________ • ____________ ____________	• Getting 0 heads.
When tossing a coin, a run occurs when two or more heads or tails occur in a row. If I toss a coin until I have one completed run, what is the probability that a run is more than three heads or tails long? E.g. run of 2: ... H T T H ... run of 3: ... T H H H T ...	____________ ____________ ____________	• ____________ ____________ • ____________ ____________	• ____________ ____________

ISBN: 9780170416023

b List the steps needed to carry out your investigation and describe how you will record your results

- You will need to describe **how** you will **perform** your investigation in enough detail that somebody else could copy it **exactly**.
- You need to describe **how** you will **record** your results.

Examples:

1 Rolling five dice at once.

Question	Description of steps and recording of results
If I roll five dice together, what is the probability that I will get fewer than two sixes?	*I will put five dice in a cup, shake them, and then tip them from a height of about 20 cm onto a table top. I will count and write down the number of sixes that appear.*

2 Kicking a rugby ball.

Question	Description of steps and recording of results
Harry has four rugby balls, and he tries to kick goals from the 22-metre line. He would like to know the probability that he gets three or four goals from each group of four attempts.	*Harry will try to kick goals with his four balls from the same spot near the 22-metre line. Then I will collect them for him and return them to the 22-metre line. We will repeat this 10 times in each session and collect the data over several sessions so that Harry doesn't get too tired. For each set of four balls, I will write down the number that go over the bar.*

ISBN: 9780170416023

Complete the table.

Question	Description of steps and recording of results
Question 1 If I roll two dice and add their numbers, what is the probability that they add to 10 or more?	
Question 2 If I have five shots at getting a netball through the hoop from just inside the circle, what is the probability that I get fewer than three through the hoop?	
I have a bag containing 10 lollies: 4 red, 3 green, 2 yellow and 1 blue. If I pick two lollies together, what is the probability that they are different colours?	
I have a bag containing 10 lollies: 4 red, 3 green, 2 yellow and 1 blue. If I pick lollies one at a time without replacement, what is the probability that I have to draw four or more lollies before I get a red one?	
When tossing a coin three times, what is the probability of getting no heads?	
When tossing a coin, a run occurs when two or more heads or tails occur in a row. If I toss a coin until I have one completed run, what is the probability that a run is more than three heads or tails long?	

ISBN: 9780170416023

c Number of trials and prediction

- You need to state the **number of trials** you will perform. There is no correct answer to this, but usually it should be at least 50, and it is a good idea to **justify** your decision.
- Doing **more trials** is likely to give you a **more reliable** estimate of the probability.
- Make a **prediction** about what your result will be. There is no correct answer for this either, but again, it is a good idea to **justify** your decision.

Examples:

1 Throwing five dice at once.

Question	Number of trials	Prediction
If I roll five dice together, what is the probability that I will get fewer than two sixes?	*I will do 80 trials because this will be quite quick to do, and I think 80 trials should give me a good estimate of the probability.*	*I think that it is quite likely that I will get 0 or 1 six, so I think the probability will be about 0.6 or 0.7.*

2 Kicking a rugby ball.

Question	Number of trials	Prediction
Harry has four rugby balls, and he tries to kick goals from the 22-metre line. He would like to know the probability that he gets three or four goals from each group of four attempts.	*I will do only 60 trials because performing each trial will take quite a lot of time, and is likely to be tiring for Harry. I think 60 trials should give me a reasonable estimate of the probability.*	*Harry is not a very experienced goal kicker, so I think the probability will be about 0.2 or 0.3.*

ISBN: 9780170416023

Complete the table and discuss your answers with your class.

Question	Number of trials	Prediction
Question 1 If I roll two dice and add their numbers, what is the probability that they add to 10 or more?		
Question 2 If I have five shots at getting a netball through the hoop from just inside the circle, what is the probability that I get fewer than three through the hoop?		
I have a bag containing 10 lollies: 4 red, 3 green, 2 yellow and 1 blue. If I pick two lollies together, what is the probability that they are different colours?		
I have a bag containing 10 lollies: 4 red, 3 green, 2 yellow and 1 blue. If I pick lollies one at a time without replacement, what is the probability that I have to draw four or more lollies before I get a red one?		
When tossing a coin three times, what is the probability of getting no heads?		
When tossing a coin, a run occurs when two or more heads or tails occur in a row. If I toss a coin until I have one completed run, what is the probability that a run is more than three heads or tails long?		

At this point your teacher will check that your plan is suitable. Then you will carry out your experiment.

ISBN: 9780170416023

2 Recording and displaying results

You need to:

- **List** your results as you collect them.
- Create a **table** to show tallies of your results, frequencies and probabilities.
- Draw a **frequency graph** to show your results.
- Draw a **probability graph** to show your results.
- Calculate the **experimental probability** for the event in your question.

Example 1

If I roll five dice together, what is the probability that I will get fewer than two sixes?

List of results: These show the number of sixes which appear each time the five dice are thrown.

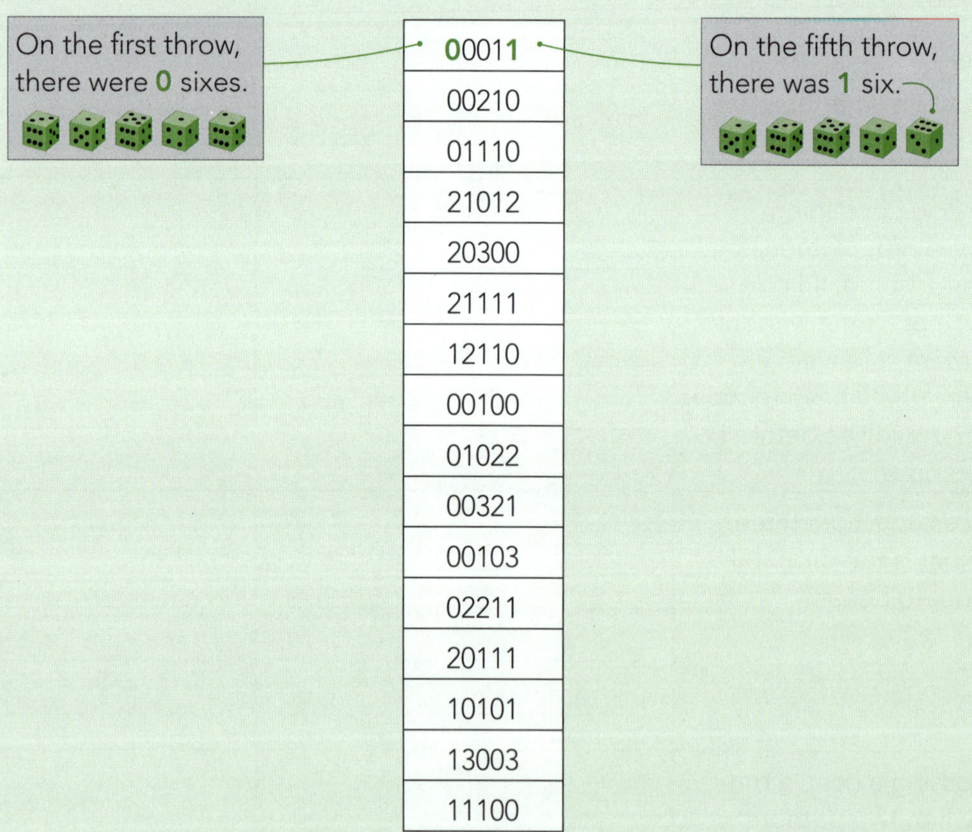

It is useful to record your results **vertically** in groups of five, particularly if you want to plot the probabilities throughout the experiment.

  ISBN: 9780170416023

Table to show tallies, frequencies and probabilities

A tally in groups of **five** makes it easy to record data as you get it, and then add it up at the end.

Before you continue, check that your frequencies **add to the number of trials**. In this case, 32 + 31 + 12 + 5 + 0 + 0 = 80.

Number of sixes	0	1	2	3	4	5	Total
Tally	𝍸 𝍸 𝍸 𝍸 𝍸 𝍸 II	𝍸 𝍸 𝍸 𝍸 𝍸 IIII I	𝍸 𝍸 II	𝍸			
Frequency	32	31	12	5	0	0	**80**
Probability	$\frac{32}{80}$	$\frac{31}{80}$	$\frac{12}{80}$	$\frac{5}{80}$	0	0	**1**
	0.4	0.3875	0.15	0.0625	0	0	**1**

'Frequency' means the number of rolls where there were, say, 0 sixes.

It's a good idea to check that your probabilities **add to 1**. In this case, 0.4 + 0.3875 + 0.15 + 0.0625 = 1.

Remember that **long run probability =** $\dfrac{\textbf{number of times an event occurs}}{\textbf{total number of trials}}$

Frequency graph

Probability graph

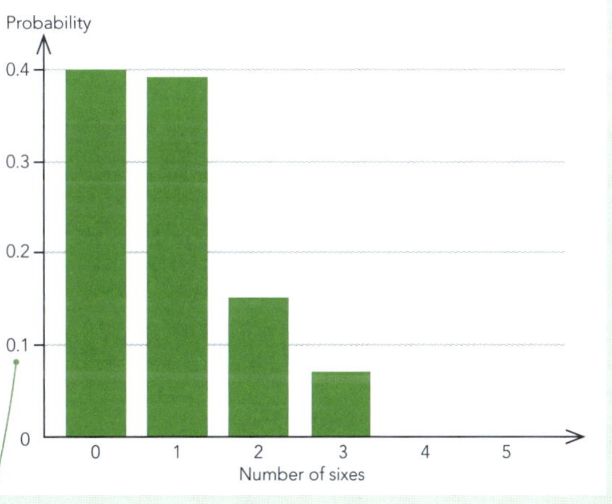

Notice that these graphs are the same shape, but have different vertical scales.

Experimental probability that I get fewer than two sixes = P(0 sixes) + P(1 six)
= 0.4 + 0.3875
= **0.7875**

ISBN: 9780170416023

Example 2

Harry has four identical rugby balls, and he tries to kick goals from the 22-metre line. He would like to know the probability that he gets three or four goals from each group of four attempts. Here are the results from 60 trials:

List of results: G means goal. N means no goal.

He kicked goals with **two** out of his first set of four rugby balls.

GNNG	NGGN	NGNN	GGNG	NNGN
NGGG	NNNN	NGGG	GNNN	GNGN
NNGN	NGNN	GGGN	NGGN	GNGG
GNNG	NNGN	GNNG	GNNG	GNNG
GNNN	GGNN	NNNG	NNGN	NGNN
NNNN	NNNG	NGNN	GNGN	GNNN
NNGG	GNNN	GNNG	GGGG	NGGN
GGGN	GNGN	GNNN	GNGG	GNGG
NGGG	GGNN	GGNG	NNGN	NGGG
NNNG	NNGN	NNGG	NGNN	NNNG
NNNG	NNGG	NNNG	GGNN	NNGG
NGNN	GNGG	NGNN	GNNN	GNNG

This data could also have been recorded in groups of five, showing just the number of goals out of each set of four attempts:

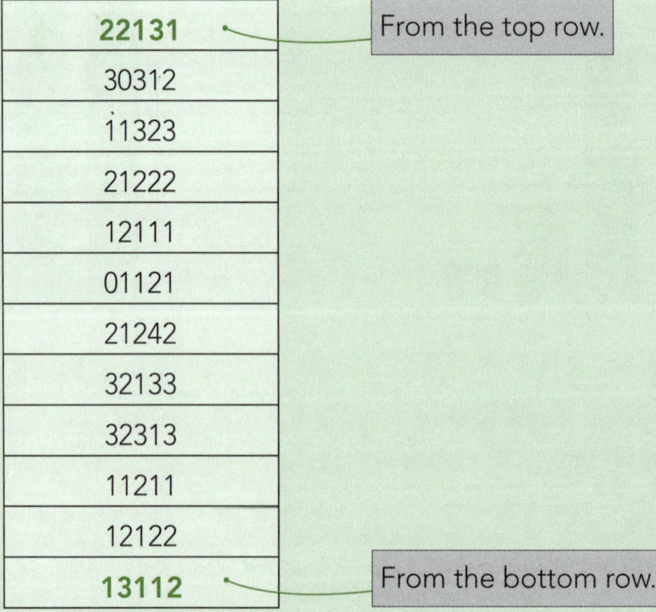

22131
30312
11323
21222
12111
01121
21242
32133
32313
11211
12122
13112

ISBN: 9780170416023

Table to show tallies, frequencies and probabilities

- This table has been made the other way around. This is particularly useful if there are a lot of different possible results.

Number of goals	Tally	Frequency	Probability	
0	II	2	$\frac{2}{60}$	$0.0\dot{3}$
1	~~IIII~~ ~~IIII~~ ~~IIII~~ ~~IIII~~ ~~IIII~~	25	$\frac{25}{60}$	$0.41\dot{6}$
2	~~IIII~~ ~~IIII~~ ~~IIII~~ ~~IIII~~	20	$\frac{20}{60}$	$0.\dot{3}$
3	~~IIII~~ ~~IIII~~ II	12	$\frac{12}{60}$	0.2
4	I	1	$\frac{1}{60}$	$0.01\dot{6}$
Total		**60**	**1**	**1**

$2 + 25 + 20 + 12 + 1 = 60$

$0.0\dot{3} + 0.41\dot{6} + 0.\dot{3} + 0.2 + 0.01\dot{6} = 1$

Frequency graph

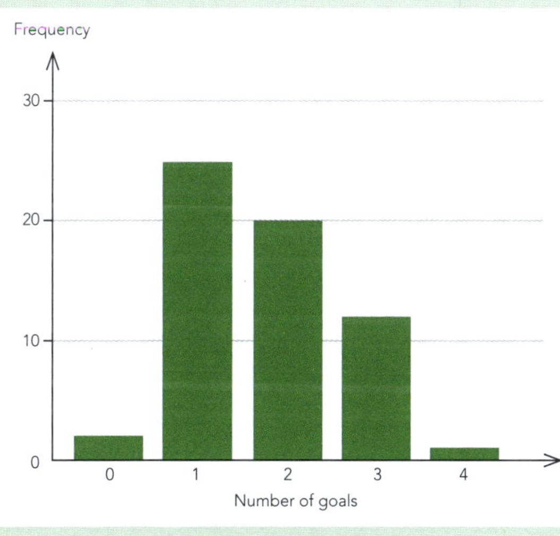

Probability graph

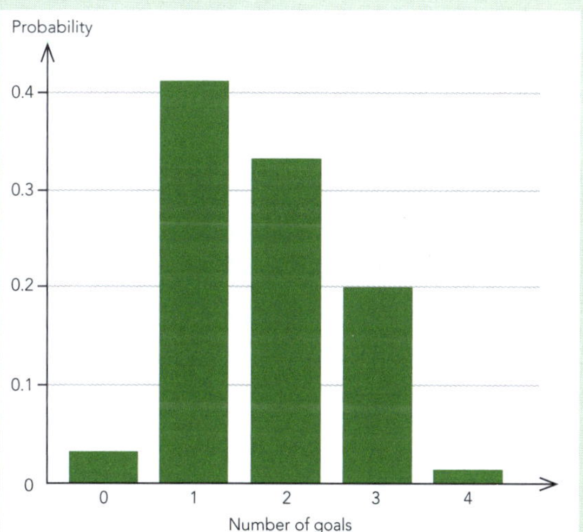

Experimental probability that Harry got three or four goals out of four

$= P(3 \text{ goals}) + P(4 \text{ goals})$

$= 0.2 + 0.01\dot{6}$

$= 0.21\dot{6}$

Answer the following.

1 If I roll two dice together and add their numbers, what is the probability that they add to 10 or more? I threw two dice 80 times and recorded the sum of the numbers each time. These are my results:

List of sums	
6 5 6 8 7	4 6 12 9 8
5 3 10 6 5	6 4 11 6 4
8 7 8 4 5	9 6 4 5 2
8 7 9 8 9	7 10 8 9 6
7 11 10 6 9	10 7 7 10 5
6 10 2 8 8	9 7 6 8 5
10 10 12 4 9	8 9 3 5 3
6 10 4 7 8	12 7 8 3 5

a Complete the table to show the probability of getting each sum.

Sum	Tally	Frequency	Probability	
2	II	2	$\frac{2}{80}$	0.025
3	IIII	4	$\frac{4}{80}$	0.05
4	~~IIII~~ II			
5	~~IIII~~ IIII			
6	~~IIII~~ ~~IIII~~ II			
7	~~IIII~~ ~~IIII~~			
8	~~IIII~~ ~~IIII~~ III			
9	~~IIII~~ IIII			
10	~~IIII~~ IIII			
11	II			
12	III			
Total		**80**	**1**	**1**

ISBN: 9780170416023

b Complete the frequency graph.

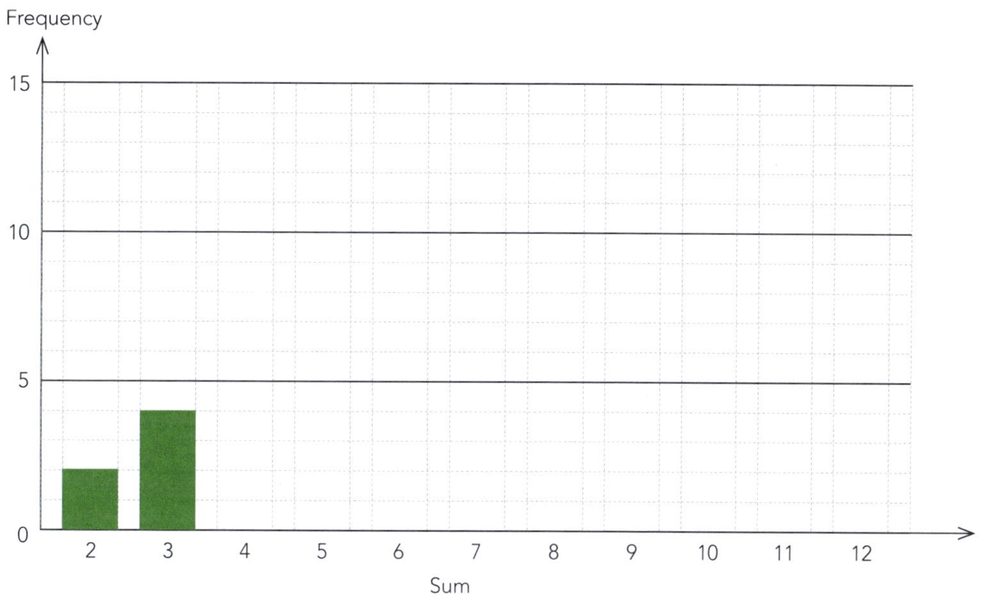

c Complete the probability graph.

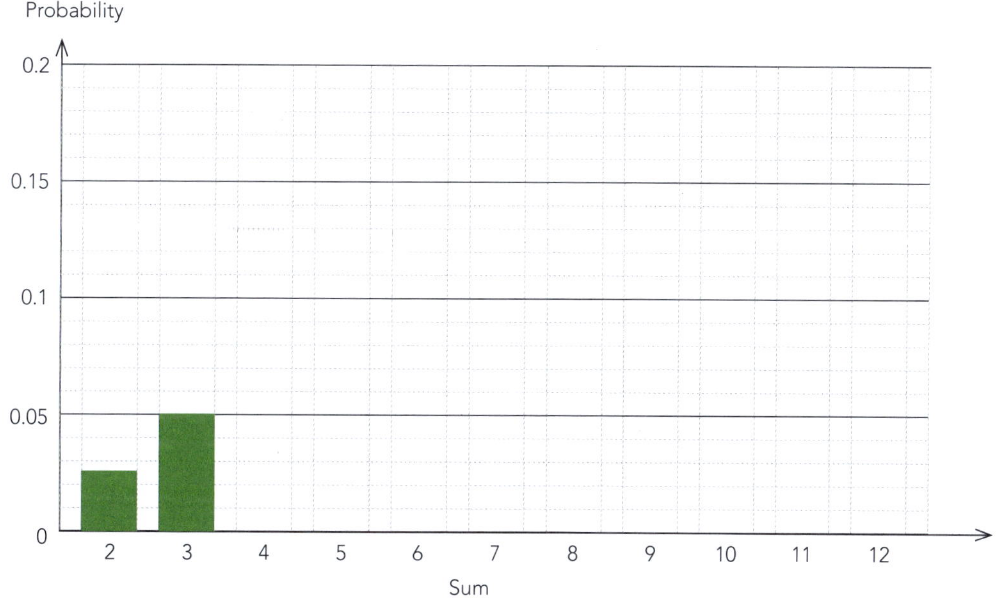

d Calculate the experimental probability that the sum added to 10 or more.

The **experimental probability** that the sum on the dice added to 10 or more

= P(10) + P(______) + P(______)

= __________ + __________ + __________

= __________

ISBN: 9780170416023

2 If I have five shots at getting a netball through the hoop from just inside the circle, what is the probability that I get fewer than three through the hoop?
I did 50 trials and recorded whether each attempt went through the hoop or not.

a **List of results:** G means the ball went through the hoop. N means it didn't.

Complete the column on the right.

					Totals for each row
GGNNG	GNGGN	NGNNG	GGGNG	NGGGG	33244
NGGGN	NNNGN	NGNNG	GNNGN	GGNGN	
NNGGN	GNGNN	GGGGN	GNGGN	GNGGG	
GGNNG	NNNGN	GNNGG	GGNNG	GNGNG	
GGNNN	GGNNG	NNGNG	GNNGN	GNGNN	
GNNNN	NGNNG	NGNNN	GNGNG	GNGNN	
NNGGG	GGNNN	GNNGG	GGGGG	NNGGN	
NGGGN	GGNGN	NGNNN	GGNGG	GNGGG	
NGGGG	GGNGN	GNGNG	GNNGN	NGGGG	
GNNNG	NNGGN	NGGGG	NGGNN	GNNNG	

b Complete the table to show the probability of getting each sum.

Number of goals			Probability	
3		17		0.34
Total		**50**		

 ISBN: 9780170416023

c Complete the frequency graph.

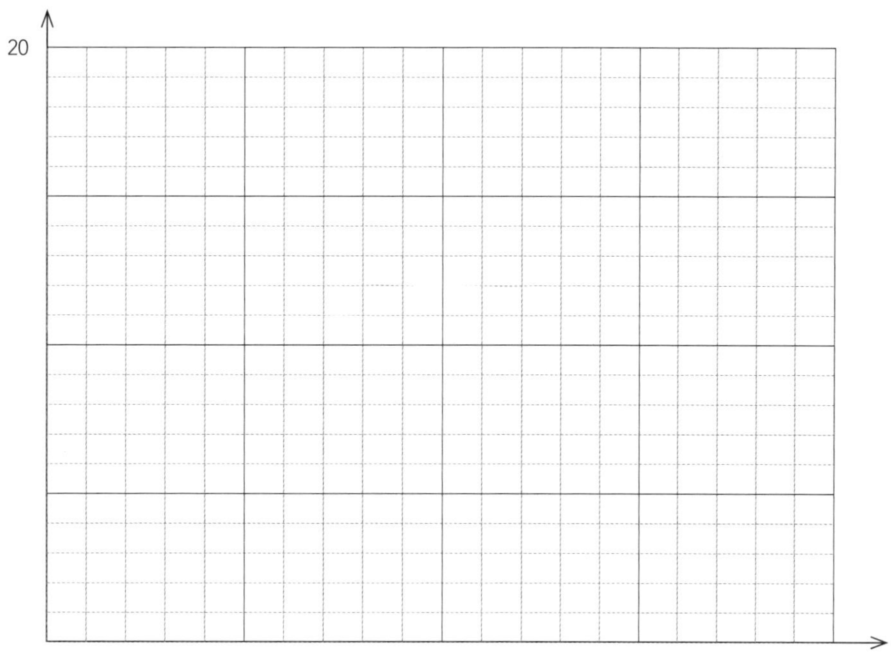

d Complete the probability graph.

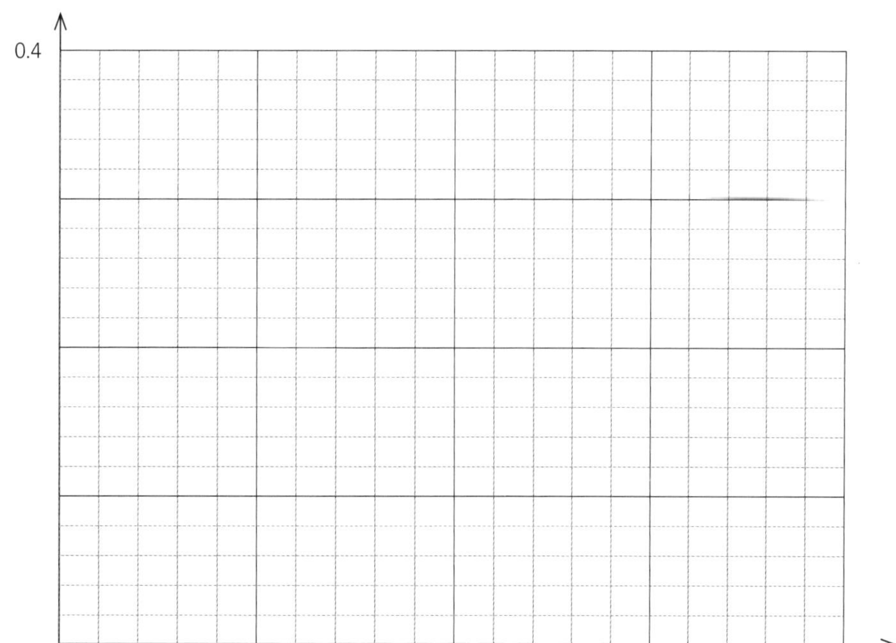

e Calculate the experimental probability.

3 Identifying patterns and discussing the data

You need to:

- Describe what you see in your **frequency and probability graphs**.

Example 1

If I roll five dice together, what is the probability that I will get fewer than two sixes? Here are the results from 80 trials:

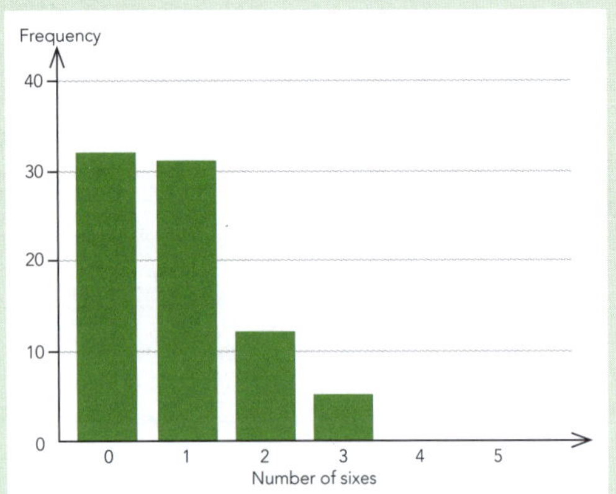

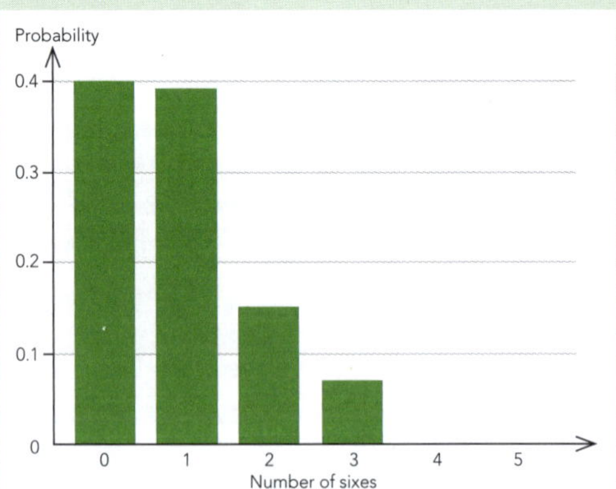

I notice that:

- *I was most likely to get no sixes or one six.*
- *The probability that I got no sixes was very similar to the probability that I got one six.*
- *I was much less likely to get two sixes and even less likely to get three.*
- *I never got four or five sixes, but I might have if I'd done more trials.*

Example 2

Harry has four rugby balls, and he tries to kick goals from the 22-metre line. He would like to know the probability that he gets three or four goals from each group of four attempts. Here are the results from 60 trials:

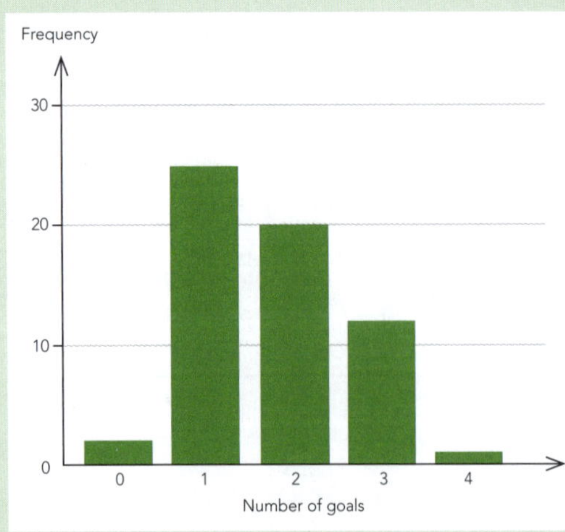

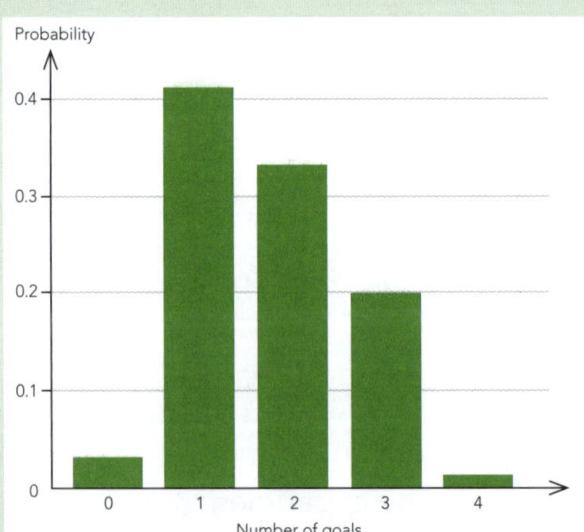

I notice that:

- *Harry was very unlikely to get no goals and even less likely to kick four goals.*
- *He was most likely to get one goal out of four tries.*
- *After one goal, the probabilities decreased as the number of goals increased.*

ISBN: 9780170416023

Describe what you see in your **frequency and probability graphs**.

1 If I roll two dice together and add their numbers, what is the probability that they add to 10 or more?

Use your graphs from page **35**.

I notice that:

-
-
-
-

2 If I have five shots at getting a netball through the hoop from just inside the circle, what is the probability that I get fewer than three through the hoop?

Use your graphs from page **37**.

ISBN: 9780170416023

4 Writing a conclusion

You need to:

- **Answer the question**.
- Compare it with your **prediction**.
- Comment on whether your experimental probability seems **reasonable**.
- List possible sources of **error**.
- Comment on the **reliability of your estimate** for the probability, and suggest how you could improve it.

Template:

The experimental probability that ______________________________ is ________.

My prediction for the probability was ________. This was **higher than/about the same as/lower than** the experimental probability.
My experimental probability seems **reasonable/surprising/unreasonable** because

____.

Possible sources of error are ____

____.

I think my estimate for the probability is **very/fairly/not very** reliable. I could improve its reliability by ____.

Example 1
If I roll five dice together, what is the probability that I will get fewer than two sixes?

- *The experimental probability that I get fewer than two sixes is 0.7825.*
- *My prediction for the probability of getting fewer than two sixes was about 0.6 or 0.7. This was lower than the experimental probability.*
- *My experimental probability seems reasonable because the probability of getting a six is only $0.1\dot{6}$, so I would expect to get 0 or 1 six most of the time.*
- *Possible sources of error are that one or more of the dice is not a fair die, and that I miscounted the number of sixes. I don't think either of these is very likely.*
- *I think my estimate for the probability is fairly reliable because I did 80 trials. I could improve its reliability by doing more trials.*

Example 2
Harry has four rugby balls, and he tries to kick goals from the 22-metre line. He would like to know the probability that he gets three or four goals from each group of four attempts.

- *The experimental probability that Harry got three or four goals is $0.21\dot{6}$.*
- *My prediction for the probability was about 0.2 or 0.3. This was about the same as the experimental probability.*
- *My experimental probability seems reasonable because it is close to my estimate and I know that Harry is not very experienced at kicking goals.*
- *Possible sources of error are that Harry didn't kick from the same spot every time, and it is also possible that his goal kicking improved throughout the experiment.*
- *I think my estimate for the probability is fairly reliable, but we did only 60 trials. We could improve its reliability by doing more trials.*

ISBN: 9780170416023

Write conclusions for each of the following.

1 If I roll two dice together and add their numbers, what is the probability that they add to 10 or more?

The experimental probability that ______________________________ is ________.

My prediction for the probability was ________. This was **higher than/about the same as/lower than** the experimental probability.

My experimental probability seems **reasonable/surprising/unreasonable** because

____

____.

Possible sources of error are ____

____

____.

I think my estimate for the probability is **very/fairly/not very** reliable. I could improve its reliability by ____.

2 If I have five shots at getting a netball through the hoop from just inside the circle, what is the probability that I get fewer than three through the hoop?

____

____

____

____

____

____

____

____

____

____

____

____

____

ISBN: 9780170416023

Optional extras

1 Plotting probabilities throughout an experiment

- During a probability experiment, it can be useful to plot the probabilities at regular intervals.
- Watching for when the graph stabilises will indicate whether you have done enough repetitions of the experiment.

You need to:
- **Calculate** the experimental probabilities as the investigation progresses.
- **Plot** these on a line graph.
- Describe and discuss what you see in the **line graph**. How do the probabilities change throughout your experiment?

Example 1
If I roll five dice together, what is the probability that I will get fewer than two sixes?
Here are the results from 80 trials:

List of results	Total number of trials	Total number of trials with fewer than two sixes	P(fewer than two sixes)	
00011	5	**5**	$\frac{5}{5}$	1
00210	10	**9**	$\frac{9}{10}$	0.9
01110	15	14	$\frac{14}{15}$	$0.9\dot{3}$
21012	20	17	$\frac{17}{20}$	0.85
20300	25	20	$\frac{20}{25}$	0.8
21111	30	24	$\frac{24}{30}$	0.8
12110	35	28	$\frac{28}{35}$	0.8
00100	40	33	$\frac{33}{40}$	0.825
01022	45	36	$\frac{36}{45}$	0.8

All five of the first five trials had fewer than two sixes.

Nine out of the first ten trials had fewer than two sixes.

If you had done only 40 trials, your experimental probability would have been 0.825.

ISBN: 9780170416023

List of results	Total number of trials	Total number of trials with fewer than two sixes	P(fewer than two sixes)	
00321	50	39	$\frac{39}{50}$	0.78
00103	55	43	$\frac{43}{55}$	$0.7\dot{8}\dot{1}$
02211	60	46	$\frac{46}{60}$	$0.7\dot{6}$
20111	65	50	$\frac{50}{65}$	0.7692
10101	70	55	$\frac{55}{70}$	0.7857
13003	75	58	$\frac{58}{75}$	$0.77\dot{3}$
11100	80	63	$\frac{63}{80}$	**0.7875**

The final probability should be the same as your experimental probability.

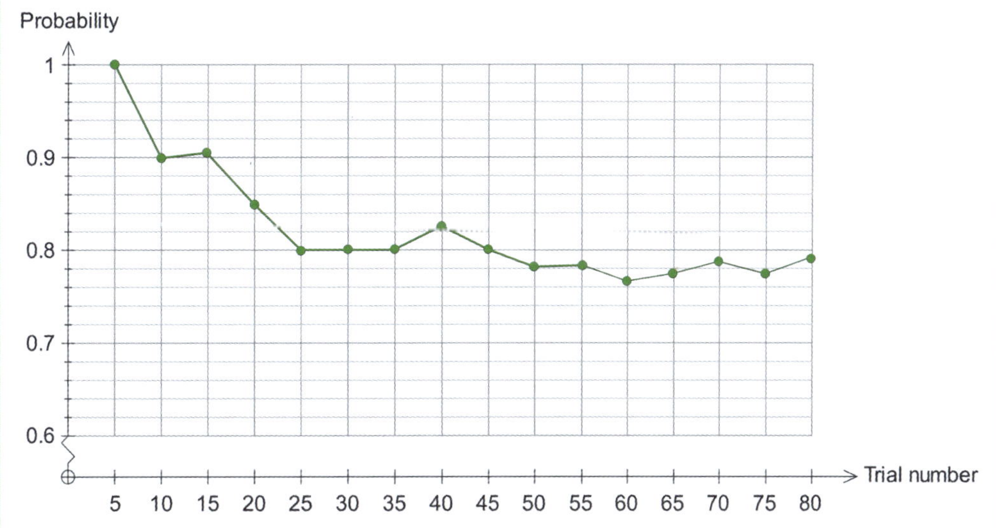

Notice that:

- There is more variation in the first 40 trials, and as the number of trials increases, the variation decreases.
- Towards the end, the graph stabilises at about 0.78.

To be **more certain** of the probability of getting fewer than two sixes when five dice are thrown, we would need to do **more trials**.

ISBN: 9780170416023

Example 2
Harry has four rugby balls, and he attempts to kick goals from the 22-metre line. He would like to know the probability that he gets three or four goals from each group of four attempts. Here are the results from 60 trials:

List of results	Total number of trials	Total number of trials where Harry kicked 3 or 4 goals	P(3 or 4 goals)	
22131	5	1	$\frac{1}{5}$	0.2
30312	10	3	$\frac{3}{10}$	0.3
11323	15	5	$\frac{5}{15}$	$0.\dot{3}$
21222	20	5	$\frac{5}{20}$	0.25
12111	25	5	$\frac{5}{25}$	0.2
01121	30	5	$\frac{5}{30}$	$0.1\dot{6}$
21242	35	6	$\frac{6}{35}$	0.1714
32133	40	9	$\frac{9}{40}$	0.225
32313	45	12	$\frac{12}{45}$	$0.2\dot{6}$
11211	50	12	$\frac{12}{50}$	0.24
12122	55	12	$\frac{12}{55}$	$0.2\dot{1}\dot{8}$
13112	60	13	$\frac{13}{60}$	$0.21\dot{6}$

ISBN: 9780170416023

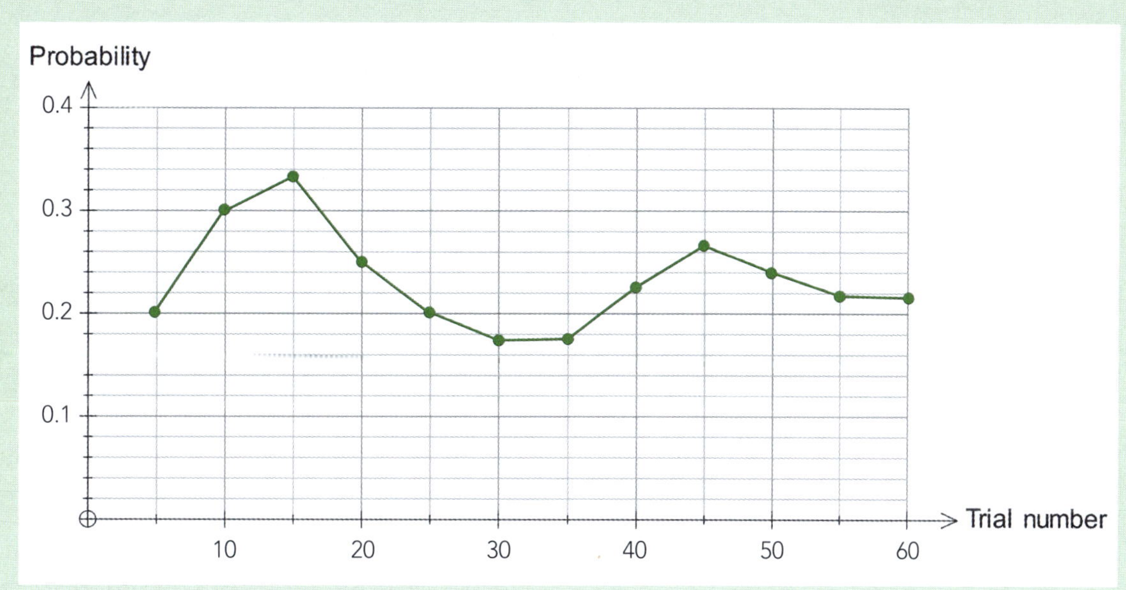

Notice that:

- There is more variation in the first 40 trials, and as the number of trials increases, the variation decreases.
- Towards the end, the graph stabilises at about 0.22.

To be **more certain** of the probability that Harry will kick three of four goals out of every four attempts, we would need to do **more trials**.

ISBN: 9780170416023

Answer the following.

1 If I roll two dice together and add their numbers, what is the probability that they add to 10 or more? I rolled two dice 80 times and recorded the sum of the number on each pair. My results are shown below.

a Complete the table in order to show the long range probability of getting 10 or more.

List of sums	Total number of trials	Total number of trials where sum is ≥ 10	P(sum is ≥ 10)	
6 5 6 8 7	5	0	$\frac{0}{5}$	0
5 3 10 6 5	10	1	$\frac{1}{10}$	0.1
8 7 8 4 5	15	1	$\frac{1}{15}$	$0.0\dot{6}$
8 7 9 8 9	20	1		
7 11 10 6 9	25	3		
6 10 2 8 8	30			
10 10 12 4 9	35			
6 10 4 7 8	40			
4 6 12 9 8	45			
6 4 11 6 4	50			
9 6 4 5 2	55			
7 10 8 9 6	60			
10 7 7 10 5	65			
9 7 6 8 5	70			
8 9 3 5 3	75			
12 7 8 3 5	80	14	$\frac{14}{80}$	0.175

ISBN: 9780170416023

b Complete the graph in order to show the long range probability of getting 10 or more.

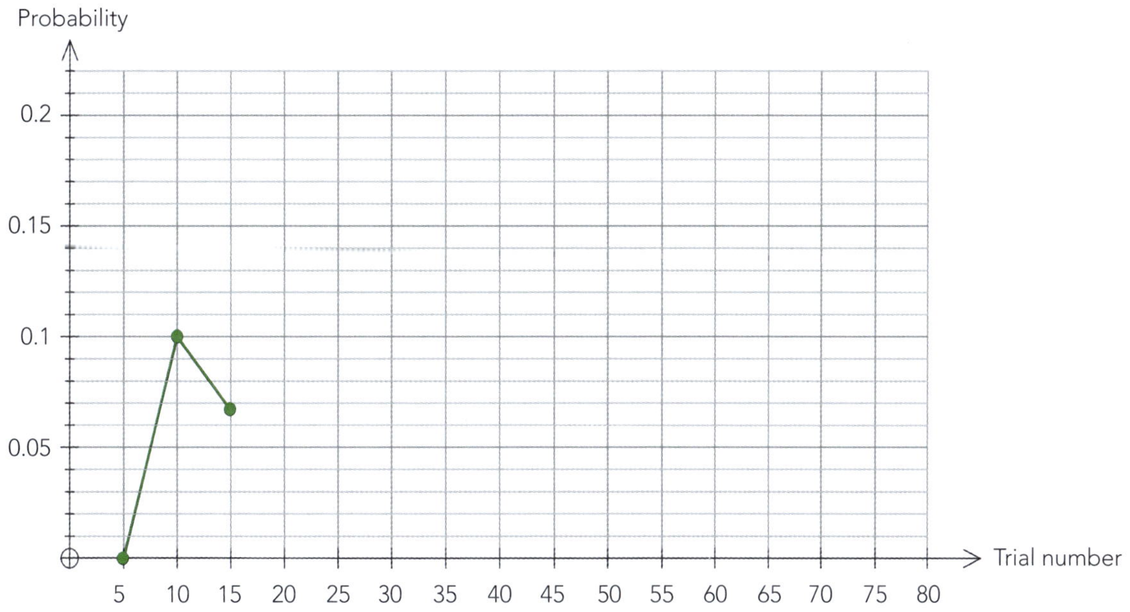

c Describe any patterns you see in the graph.

____

____

____

____

d Based on this experiment, what is the probability that the sum on the next pair of dice that I throw will be 10 or more?

____

____

e How certain can I be of this probability?

____

____

f Describe what I should do in order to get a better estimate of the probability.

____

____

____

2 If I have five shots at getting a netball through the hoop from just inside the circle, what is the probability that I get fewer than three through the hoop?
I did 50 trials and recorded whether each attempt went through the hoop or not. My results are shown below.

a Complete the table in order to show the long range probability that I get fewer than three through the hoop.

Number of goals	Total number of trials	Total number of trials with 0, 1 or 2 goals	P(0, 1 or 2 goals)	
33244	5	1	$\frac{1}{5}$	0.2
31223	10	4		
22434	15			
31333	20			
23222	25			
12132	30			
32352	35			
33144	40			
43324	45			
22322	50			0.46

 ISBN: 9780170416023

b Complete the graph in order to show the long range probability of getting fewer than three through the hoop.

c Discuss what these results tell you.

3 According to Murphy's law, if you drop a drawing pin while walking around in bare feet, the drawing pin usually lands point-side up. Ruby would like to investigate this. She takes 10 drawing pins, drops them onto the floor from the height of the table, and counts the number that land point-side up. The results of her first 150 trials are shown below.

a Complete the table.

Total number of drawing pins dropped	Number in each trial landing with point up	Total number that have landed point up	P(pins land point up)	
10	5			
20	6			
30	6			
40	7			
50	5			
60	4			
70	4			
80	6			
90	8			
100	5			
110	8			
120	10			
130	4			
140	7			
150	6			

  ISBN: 9780170416023

b Complete the graph.

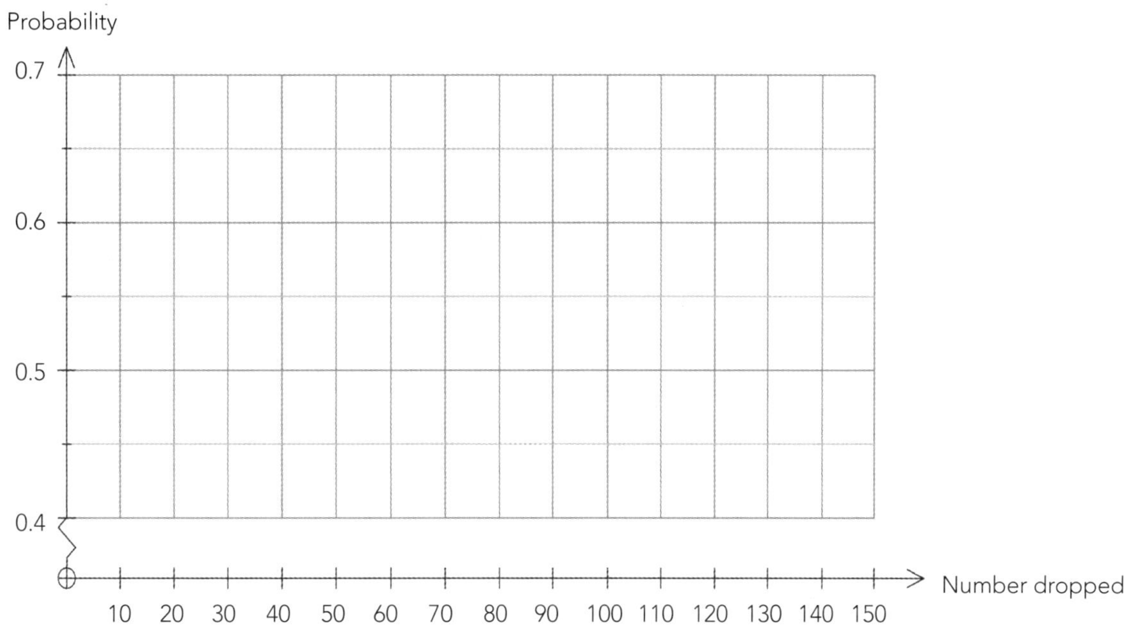

c Discuss what these results tell you.

4 Also according to Murphy's law, if you drop a piece of buttered toast, it will land buttered-side down. Ngaire wanted to know whether this is true for toast with jam. She conducted an experiment in which she dropped pieces of toast spread with jam and recorded whether the jam side was 'down' or 'up' when they landed. The results for her first 20 trials are shown below.

a Complete the table.

Trial number	Result	Total 'down'	P('down')	
1	down			
2	up			
3	down			
4	down			
5	up			
6	down			
7	up			
8	up			
9	up			
10	down			
11	down			
12	down			
13	up			
14	down			
15	up			
16	down			

ISBN: 9780170416023

Trial number	Result	Total 'down'	P('down')	
17	down			
18	up			
19	down			
20	down			

b Complete the graph.

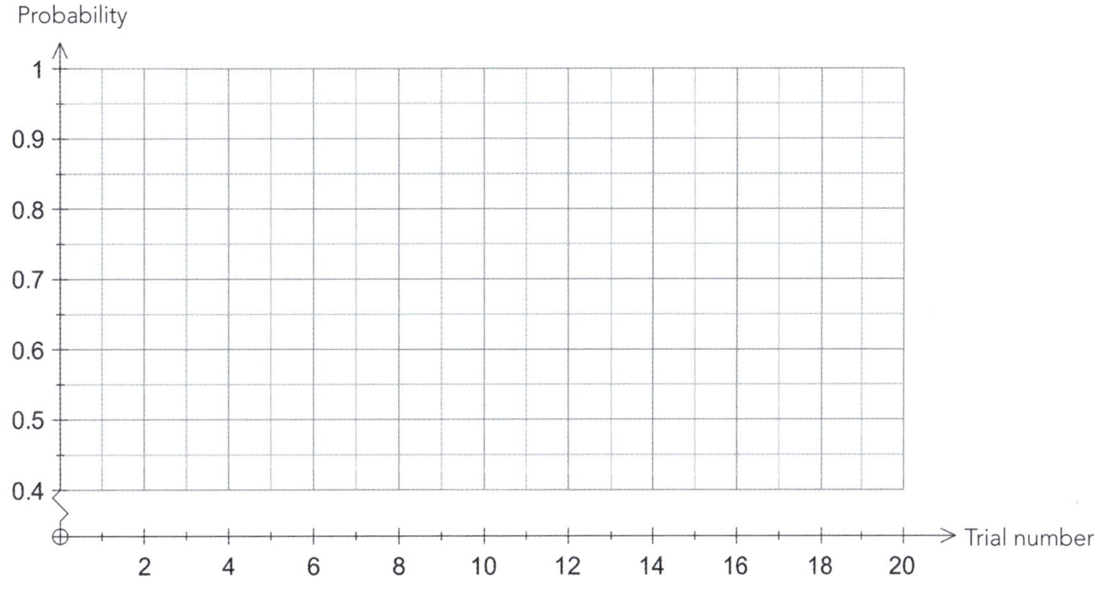

c Discuss what these results tell you.

2 Calculating the theoretical probability

- For some experiments you can calculate the theoretical probability.
- Experiments in which you **can** calculate theoretical probabilities are usually those involving equally likely outcomes (dice, coins, lollies which are identical apart from their colour, etc.).
- Experiments in which you **cannot** calculate theoretical probabilities tend to be those involving skills (such as kicking a rugby ball), natural events (such as thunderstorms), etc.

You should:
- **Show** how you calculated the theoretical probability.
- **Compare** your experimental probability with the theoretical probability.
- **Discuss**, including why they might be similar or different.

Example 1
If I roll five dice together, what is the probability that I will get fewer than two sixes?
The experimental probability was 0.7875.

For this calculation, imagine that the dice are different colours: green, red, yellow, blue and white.

Calculation of the theoretical probability:

Because the probability of getting a six is $\frac{1}{6}$, the probability of getting a 'not six' is $\frac{5}{6}$.

'Fewer than two sixes' means 0 sixes or 1 six:

P(0 sixes) $= \frac{5}{6} \times \frac{5}{6} \times \frac{5}{6} \times \frac{5}{6} \times \frac{5}{6} = \mathbf{0.4019}$

P(the **green** die is a six) $= \frac{1}{6} \times \frac{5}{6} \times \frac{5}{6} \times \frac{5}{6} \times \frac{5}{6}$

However, **any** of the **five** dice could be the one showing a six.

$\therefore$ **P(1 six)** $= \mathbf{5} \times \frac{1}{6} \times \frac{5}{6} \times \frac{5}{6} \times \frac{5}{6} \times \frac{5}{6} = \mathbf{0.4019}$

Add these.

So the theoretical probability of throwing fewer than two sixes = 0.4019 + 0.4019
= **0.8038**.

Comparison with the experimental probability and discussion:

The experimental probability was 0.7875, which is a little lower than 0.8038. I did 80 trials, which is a reasonable number. However, I would expect the experimental probability would have been even closer to 0.8038 if I had done more trials.

ISBN: 9780170416023

Example 2

Harry has four rugby balls, and he attempts to kick goals from the 22-metre line. He would like to know the probability that he gets three or four goals from each group of four attempts. Here are the results from 60 trials:

This is an example of an experiment for which the theoretical probability cannot be calculated because we do not know the probability that Harry kicks a single goal.

Example 3

When tossing a coin three times, what is the probability of getting no heads?
Eighty trials were performed. The experimental probability was 0.15.

Calculation of the theoretical probability:

$$\text{P(head)} = \frac{1}{2} \text{ and P(tail)} = \frac{1}{2}$$

$$\begin{aligned}\text{P(no heads)} &= \text{P(tail)} \times \text{P(tail)} \times \text{P(tail)} \\ &= \frac{1}{2} \times \frac{1}{2} \times \frac{1}{2} \\ &= \frac{1}{8} \text{ or } 0.125\end{aligned}$$

Comparison with the experimental probability and discussion:

The experimental probability was 0.15, which is a little higher than 0.125. I did 80 trials, which is a reasonable number. However, I would expect the experimental probability would have been even closer to 0.125 if I had done more trials.

ISBN: 9780170416023

Calculate theoretical probabilities for the following situations, and compare each with the given experimental probabilities.

1 If I roll two dice together and add their numbers, what is the probability that they add to 10 or more? I threw two dice 80 times.

The experimental probability was 0.175.

Calculation of the theoretical probability:

Comparison with the experimental probability, and discussion:

2 I have a bag containing 8 lollies which are the same apart from their colour. There are 2 red lollies and 6 green ones. I take one lolly from the bag and eat it, and then I take a second lolly. I would like to know the probability that the two lollies are different colours. Sixty trials were done (without actually eating the lollies).

The experimental probability was 0.39.

Calculation of the theoretical probability:

Comparison with the experimental probability and discussion:

ISBN: 9780170416023

3 If I toss a coin and throw one die, what is the probability that I get a head with a 5 or a 6?

One hundred trials were done. The experimental probability was 0.19.

Calculation of the theoretical probability:

Comparison with the experimental probability, and discussion:

____

____

____

____

____

4 Jamie's little sister is colouring in a pattern. She has six pencils which are the same apart from their colour: two different shades of red, two of blue and two of yellow. She closes her eyes and selects one pencil and completes half of the pattern. She replaces the pencil, and then selects a second pencil to complete the pattern. Jamie would like to know the probability that she selects a red or blue pencil for the first half, and a yellow pencil for completing the rest.

She borrows the pencils and does 50 trials. The experimental probability was 0.26.

Calculation of the theoretical probability:

Comparison with the experimental probability, and discussion:

____

____

____

____

____

ISBN: 9780170416023

Putting it all together

You will need to do the following:

Plan your investigation

- Pose an appropriate **question**.
- List all the possible **outcomes**. These must relate to the question.
- State the **event** you are interested in.
- **List the steps** needed to carry out your investigation and **describe** how you will record your results.
- State the **number** of trials you will perform, or the **number** of observations you will make.
- Make a **prediction**.

Record, display and analyse your results

- **List** your results as you collect them.
- Create a **table** to show tallies of your results, frequencies and probabilities.
- Draw a **frequency graph** to show your results.
- Draw a **probability graph** to show your results.
- Calculate the **experimental probability** for the event in your question.

Identify patterns and discuss the data

- Describe what you see in your **frequency and probability graphs**.

Write a conclusion

- **Answer the question**.
- Compare it with your **prediction**.
- Does your experimental probability seem **reasonable**?
- List possible sources of **error**.
- Comment on the **reliability of your estimate** for the probability, and suggest how you could improve it.

Optional extras:

1 Plot the probabilities throughout the experiment.
   - **Calculate** the experimental probabilities as the investigation progresses.
   - **Plot** these on a line graph.
   - **Describe** and **discuss** what you see in the line graph. How do the probabilities change throughout your experiment?

2 Calculate the theoretical probability (not always possible).
   - **Show** how you calculated the experimental probability.
   - **Compare** your experimental probability with the theoretical probability.
   - **Discuss**, including why they might be similar or different.

ISBN: 9780170416023

Annotated example

If I roll three dice together, what is the probability that exactly two dice show the same number? There will be two possible outcomes in my experiment:

✓ Question

1 *I will get exactly two dice with the same number, or*
2 *I will get none with the same number or three with the same number.*

✓ Outcomes

The event I am interested in is getting exactly two with the same number.

✓ Event

I will roll three dice together 60 times, and for each roll I will write down how many dice show the same number.

✓ Steps and recording of results
✓ Number of trials

I think that I will get two of the same number in about half the trials.

✓ Prediction

List of results	Total number of trials	Total number of trials with two dice the same	P(two the same)	
02002	5	2	$\frac{2}{5}$	0.4
20200	10	4	$\frac{4}{10}$	0.4
22022	15	8	$\frac{8}{15}$	$0.5\dot{3}$
20200	20	10	$\frac{10}{20}$	0.5
02023	25	12	$\frac{12}{25}$	0.48
20002	30	14	$\frac{14}{30}$	$0.4\dot{6}$
02220	35	17	$\frac{17}{35}$	0.4857
00002	40	18	$\frac{18}{40}$	0.45
00000	45	18	$\frac{18}{45}$	0.4
00222	50	21	$\frac{21}{50}$	0.42
00022	55	23	$\frac{23}{55}$	$0.4\dot{1}\dot{8}$
22222	60	28	$\frac{28}{60}$	$0.4\dot{6}$

✓ List of results
✓ Table with frequencies and probabilities

ISBN: 9780170416023

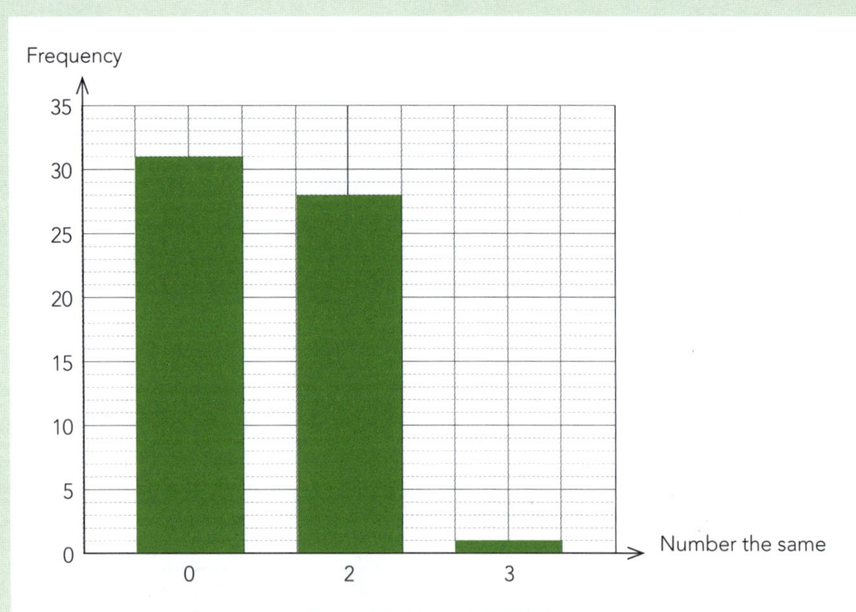

✓ Frequency graph

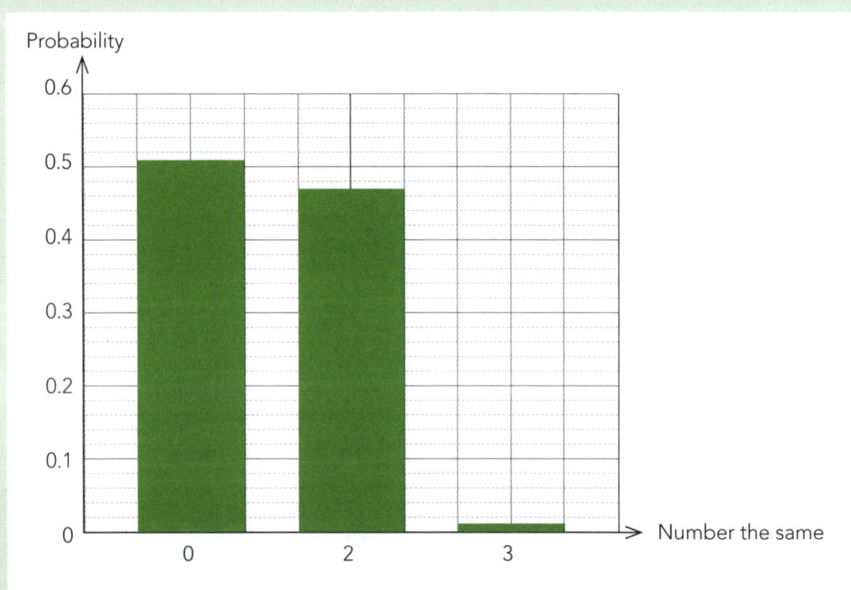

✓ Probability graph

Experimental probability of getting two dice the same $= \frac{28}{60} = 0.4\dot{6}$.

✓ Probability calculation

The graphs show me that I was most likely to get no dice the same, I was slightly less likely to get two dice the same, and very unlikely to get three dice the same.

✓ Graph discussion

ISBN: 9780170416023

Optional extra 1

Plot of probabilities throughout the experiment:

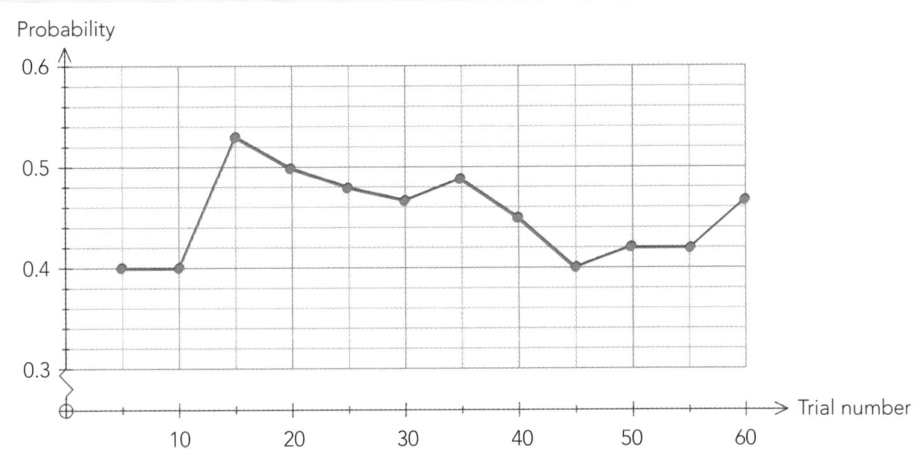

I notice that the graph was variable at the start, jumping from 0.4 to 0.53 between the tenth and fifteenth trial. I would have expected it to be smoother towards the right, but a long run with only one trial with two dice the same between trials 35 and 47, and another run of seven trials with two dice the same at the end, meant that it did not stabilise as I would have expected. This suggests that in order to get a more reliable estimate of the probability, I should do more trials, say 100.

Optional extra 2

Calculation of the theoretical probabilities:

P(getting no dice the same) $= 1 \times \frac{5}{6} \times \frac{4}{6} = \frac{20}{36} = 0.\dot{5}$

P(getting three dice the same) $= 1 \times \frac{1}{6} \times \frac{1}{6} = \frac{1}{36} = 0.02\dot{7}$

Since there are only three possibilities (getting 0, 2 or 3 the same),

P(two dice the same) $= 1 - 0.\dot{5} - 0.2\dot{7}$

$= 0.41\dot{6}$

My experimental probability was 0.46, which is a little higher than the theoretical probability. It would probably be closer if I had done more trials.

I found that my experimental probability for getting exactly two dice the same when rolling three at once was 0.46, which was a little lower than my estimate of 0.5. Since I now know that the theoretical probability is $0.41\dot{6}$*, my estimate was a bit high. However, because I did only 60 trials, I think my experimental probability was reasonable, but could be improved by doing more trials. Assuming that the dice I used were fair, and that I counted correctly, I don't think there were any sources of error in this experiment.*

✓ Answer to question
✓ Comparison with estimate
✓ Reasonable estimate?
✓ Improvement
✓ Sources of error

Practice tasks

Practice task one

Card game

This activity requires you to write a report about a statistical investigation into a game of chance. You will be assessed on the quality of your discussion and reasoning and how well you link this to the context.

Investigation: Huia is planning a game of chance for the school fair. She has created six cards. Four show turtles and two show ruru (moreporks).

She will:

- turn the cards face down
- ask the player to pick up one card, and keep it in their hand
- then pick a second card.

She will give a prize to the player if they have picked one of each design.

In order to decide the value of the prize, she needs to know the probability of a player picking one of each design. She decides that the best way of doing this is to pretend she is a player and do 60 trials of the game.

She recorded just the number of ruru picked up. Her results, in groups of five, are shown at the right.

This task requires you to write a report on this investigation for Huia.

Number of ruru
02010
11101
00111
10011
10110
01110
12100
01001
00111
01211
11101
21001

  ISBN: 9780170416023

Plan of investigation

Question: ____________________

____

Outcomes: 1 ____________________ 2 ____________________

Event of interest: ____________________

List of the steps she could have used to carry out the investigation:

____

____

____

Explanation of how her results might have been recorded:

____

____

Number of trials/observations: ____________________

You make a prediction: ____________________

Record, display and analysis of results

Table showing results, frequencies and probabilities:

Number of ruru	Total number of trials	Total number with exactly one of each design	P(one of each)	
02010	5			
11101	10			
00111	15			
10011	20			
10110	25			
01110	30			
12100	35			
01001	40			
00111	45			
01211	50			
11101	55			
21001	60			

ISBN: 9780170416023

Frequency graph:

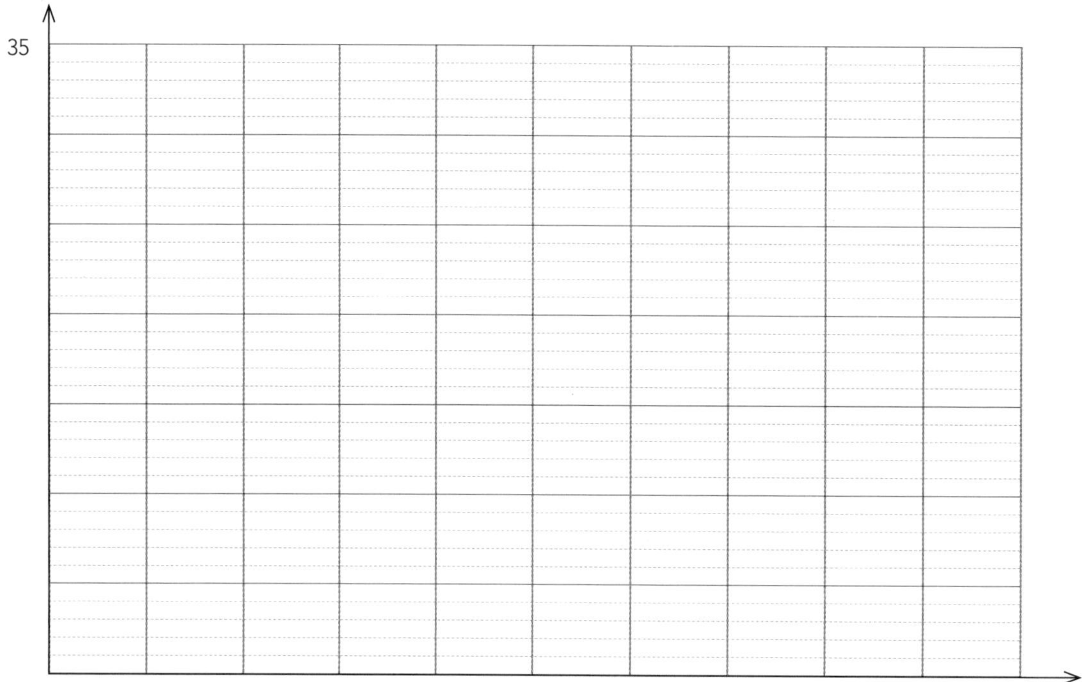

Probability graph:

ISBN: 9780170416023

Calculation of experimental probability:

Identify patterns and discuss the data

Conclusion

Answer to the question:

Comparison with prediction:

Does the experimental probability seem reasonable?

Possible sources of error:

Comment on the reliability of the estimate for the probability, and suggestions for how it could be improved.

ISBN: 9780170416023

Optional extras:

1 Plot of the probabilities throughout the experiment

Calculation of the experimental probabilities: See table on page 63.

Line graph of probabilities

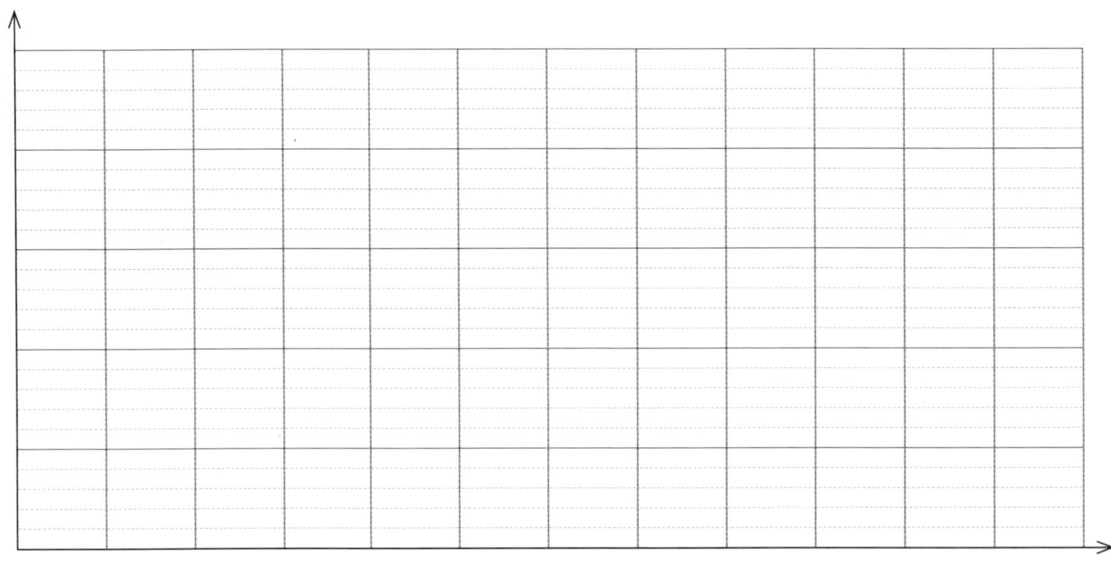

Discussion:

2 Calculation of the theoretical probability

Calculations:

Comparison with the experimental probability and discussion:

 ISBN: 9780170416023

Practice task two

Paper planes

This activity requires you to undertake a statistical investigation into an activity involving chance.

You will be assessed on the quality of your discussion and reasoning and how well you link this to the context.

Tane's class are making paper aeroplanes and each class member will have three throws of their plane in a final competition. The planes will be judged using several criteria. One of those is the number of times the plane travels at least 5 metres before hitting the ground.

Tane would like to know the probability that his plane goes at least 5 metres before hitting the ground in all three of his throws, so he carries out an experiment at home. He thinks the probability that, with his latest design, he can get all three throws to travel at least 5 metres will be at least 0.5. He does 50 trials. In each he throws his plane three times, and he records the number of times it goes at least 5 metres.

You can

- either use the data below to write a report for Tane, and mark it using the answers in the back of the book,
- or collect your own data and get your teacher to check your report.

You need to include the following in your report:

- *Plan of investigation*
  - Question
  - Outcomes
  - Event of interest
  - List of the steps needed to carry out the investigation
  - Explanation of how the results will be recorded
  - Number of trials/observations
  - Prediction
- *Record, display and analysis of results*
  - List of results
  - Table showing results, frequencies and probabilities
  - Frequency graph
  - Probability graph
  - Calculation of experimental probability
- *Identify patterns and discuss the data*
- *Conclusion*
  - Answer to the question
  - Comparison with prediction
  - Does the experimental probability seem reasonable?
  - Possible sources of error
  - Comment on the reliability of the estimate for the probability, and suggestions for how it could be improved.

Relate your comments about the distribution, and the information presented in your displays, to the context.

Optional extra: Plot of the probabilities throughout the experiment.

ISBN: 9780170416023

Tane's data

Number over 5 m	Total number of trials
22313	5
11233	10
21032	15
13211	20
23301	25
02321	30
33221	35
30121	40
32022	45
22321	50

Plan of investigation

ISBN: 9780170416023

Record, display and analysis of results

Number over 5 m	Total number of trials			
22313	5			
11233	10			
21032	15			
13211	20			
23301	25			
02321	30			
33221	35			
30121	40			
32022	45			
22321	50			

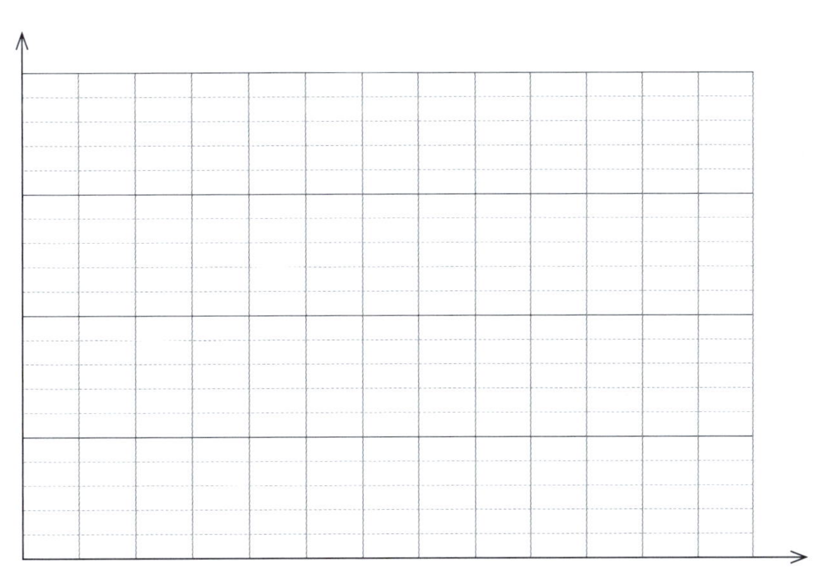

ISBN: 9780170416023

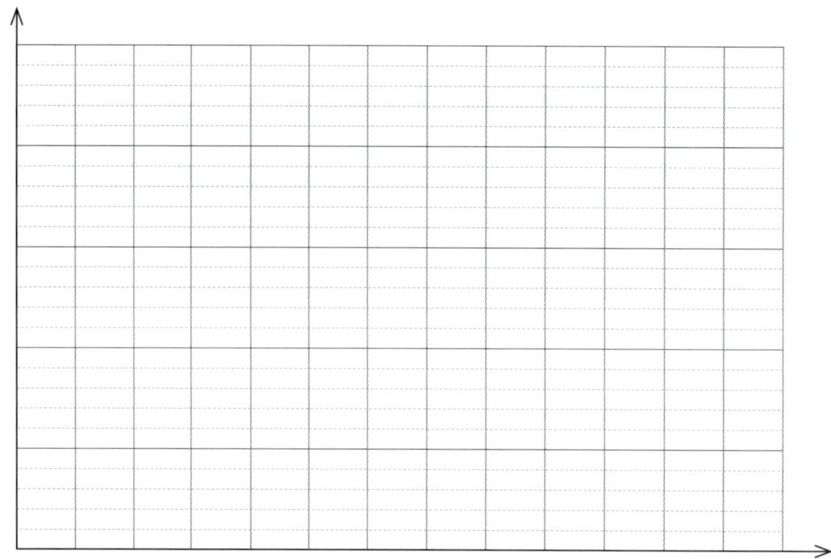

Identify patterns and discuss the data

Conclusion

  ISBN: 9780170416023

Optional extra: Plot of the probabilities throughout the experiment

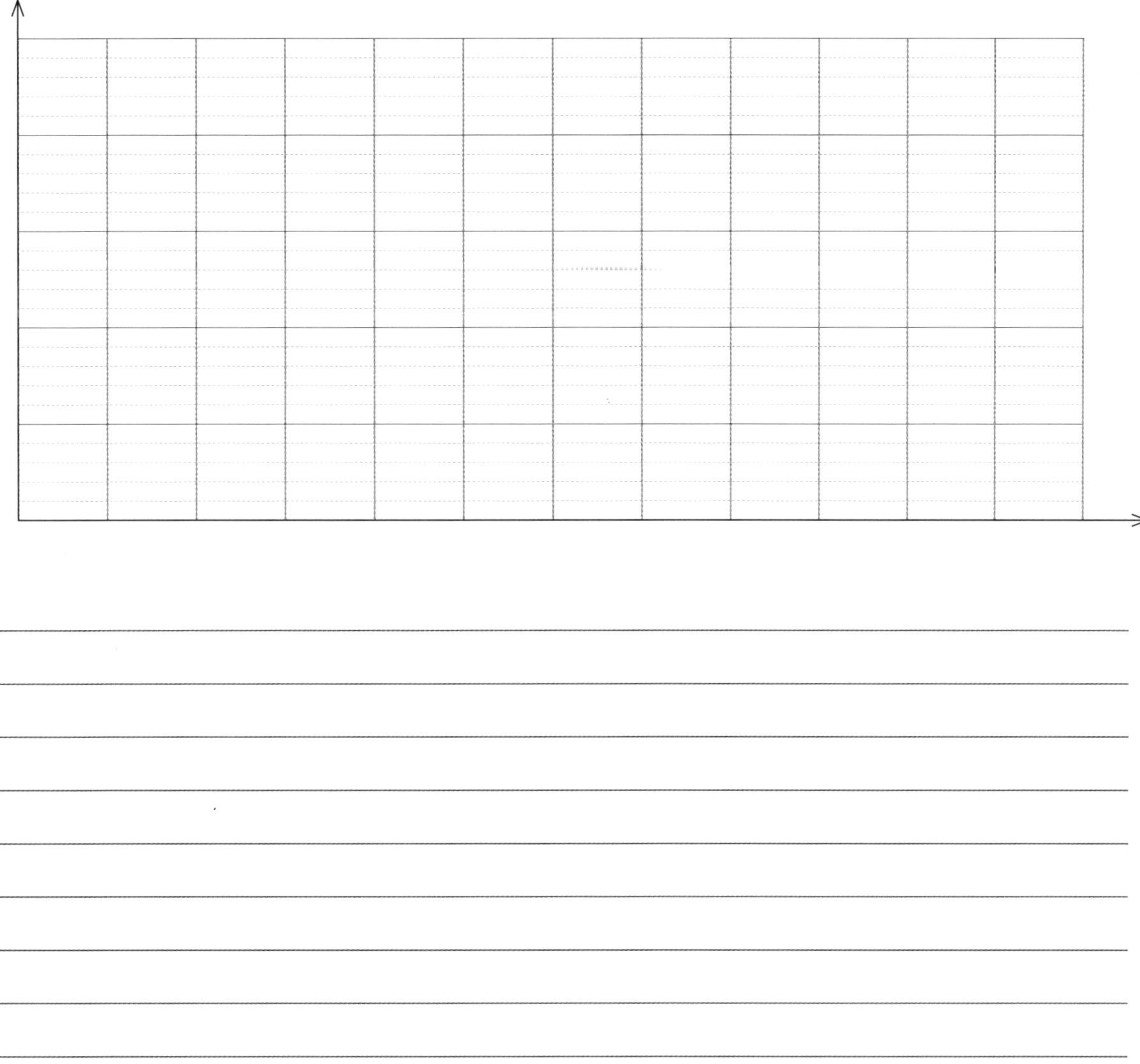

Practice task three

Bottle flip

This activity requires you to undertake a statistical investigation into an activity involving chance.

You will be assessed on the quality of your discussion and reasoning and how well you link this to the context.

Task

Pose an investigative question involving the game bottle flip. In this game a bottle containing some liquid is flipped vertically through 360°, with the object of making it land the right way up. A suitable investigative question reflects the probability situation, has a clear variable for investigation, requires statistical analysis, and can be meaningfully answered with data gathered.

You must include the following in your report:

- *Plan of investigation*
  - Question
  - Outcomes
  - Event of interest
  - List of the steps needed to carry out the investigation
  - Explanation of how the results will be recorded
  - Number of trials/observations
  - Prediction
- *Record, display and analysis of results*
  - List of results
  - Table showing results, frequencies and probabilities
  - Frequency graph
  - Probability graph
  - Calculation of experimental probability
- *Identify patterns and discuss the data*
- *Conclusion*
  - Answer to the question
  - Comparison with prediction
  - Does the experimental probability seem reasonable?
  - Possible sources of error
  - Comment on the reliability of the estimate for the probability, and suggestions for how it could be improved.

Relate your comments about the distribution, and the information presented in your displays, to the context.

Optional extras:

1. Plot of the probabilities throughout the experiment
2. Calculation of the theoretical probability

ISBN: 9780170416023

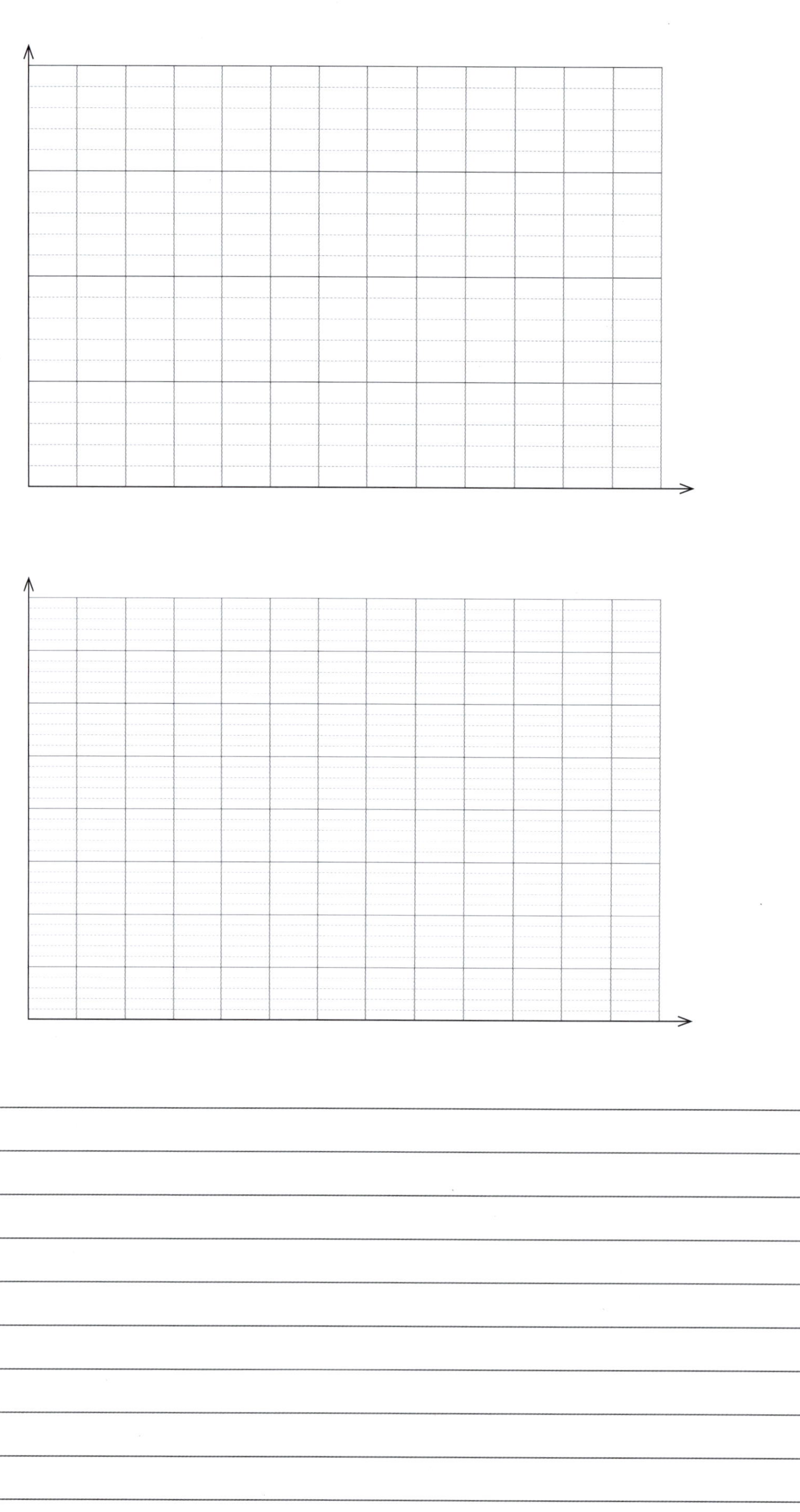

 ISBN: 9780170416023

Answers

Probability (pp. 6–23)

The range of values for probabilities (p. 6)

0	impossible, no chance, no way
0.1	very unlikely, slight chance, possible
0.2	improbable, possible, unlikely
0.3	improbable, maybe, possible, unlikely
0.4	maybe, possible, unlikely
0.5	maybe, possible, fifty fifty
0.6	likely, probable
0.7	likely, probable
0.8	very likely, probable
0.9	very likely, extremely likely
1.0	definite, a sure thing

Using numbers for writing probabilities (p. 7)

1 $\frac{7}{16} = 0.4375$ $\frac{1}{3} = 0.\dot{3}$ Most likely: $\frac{7}{16}$

2 $\frac{3}{4} = 0.75$ $\frac{8}{11} = 0.\dot{7}\dot{2}$ Most likely: $\frac{3}{4}$

3 $\frac{17}{18} = 0.9\dot{4}$ $\frac{19}{20} = 0.95$ Most likely: $\frac{19}{20}$

4 $\frac{13}{24} = 0.541\dot{6}$ $\frac{27}{50} = 0.54$ Most likely: $\frac{13}{24}$

5 $\frac{11}{20} = 0.55$ $\frac{7}{13} = 0.5385$ Most likely: $\frac{11}{20}$

6 $\frac{6}{17} = 0.3529$ $\frac{3}{8} = 0.375$ Most likely: $\frac{3}{8}$

Test yourself (p. 7)

1 ✓ = 0.05 which is between 0 and 1, so it is a valid probability.

2 ✓ Half the time means p = 0.5 which is between 0 and 1, so it is a valid probability.

3 × 110% means p = 1.1. Probabilities greater than 1 are not possible.

4 × –0.1 is negative, and negative probabilities do not exist.

Ways of calculating probabilities (pp. 8–13)

1 Equally likely outcomes (pp. 8–11)

With a single event (pp. 8–9)

1 $\frac{1}{6} = 0.1\dot{6}$ **2** $\frac{3}{6} = 0.5$

3 $\frac{3}{6} = 0.5$ **4** $\frac{5}{6} = 0.8\dot{3}$

5 $\frac{4}{6} = 0.\dot{6}$ **6** $\frac{0}{6} = 0$

7 $\frac{6}{6} = 1$ **8** $\frac{1}{6} = 0.1\dot{6}$

9 $\frac{2}{6} = 0.\dot{3}$ **10** $\frac{3}{6} = 0.5$

11 $\frac{3}{6} = 0.5$ **12** $\frac{0}{6} = 0$

13 $\frac{5}{6} = 0.8\dot{3}$ **14** $\frac{1}{6} = 0.1\dot{6}$

15 $\frac{7}{24} = 0.291\dot{6}$ **16** $\frac{17}{24}$ or $1 - 0.291\dot{6} = 0.708\dot{3}$

17 $\frac{10}{24} = 0.41\dot{6}$ **18** $\frac{14}{24}$ or $1 - 0.41\dot{6} = 0.58\dot{3}$

19 $\frac{19}{24} = 0.791\dot{6}$ **20** $\frac{19}{24} = 0.791\dot{6}$

21 $\frac{0}{24} = 0$ **22** $\frac{24}{24} = 1$

23 $\frac{1}{28} = 0.0357$ **24** $\frac{7}{28} = 0.25$

25 $\frac{1}{28} = 0.0357$ **26** $\frac{6}{28} = 0.2143$

27 $\frac{3}{28} = 0.1071$

Combining two events (pp. 10–11)

1

	1	2	3	4	5	6
1	1 1	1 2	1 3	1 4	1 5	1 6
2	2 1	2 2	2 3	2 4	2 5	2 6
3	3 1	3 2	3 3	3 4	3 5	3 6
4	4 1	4 2	4 3	4 4	4 5	4 6
5	5 1	5 2	5 3	5 4	5 5	5 6
6	6 1	6 2	6 3	6 4	6 5	6 6

2 36 **3** (2, 1) and (1, 2)

4 $\frac{2}{36} = 0.0\dot{5}$ **5** $\frac{4}{36} = 0.\dot{1}$

6 $\frac{6}{36} = 0.1\dot{6}$ **7** $\frac{3}{36} = 0.08\dot{3}$

8 $1 - 0.08\dot{3}$ or $\frac{33}{36} = 0.91\dot{6}$

9 $\frac{18}{36} = 0.5$ **10** $\frac{6}{36} = 0.1\dot{6}$

11 $\frac{15}{36} = 0.41\dot{6}$

ISBN: 9780170416023

12

	1	2	3	4	5	6
1	1 1	1 2	1 3	1 4	1 5	1 6
2	2 1	2 2	2 3	2 4	2 5	2 6
4	4 1	4 2	4 3	4 4	4 5	4 6
8	8 1	8 2	8 3	8 4	8 5	8 6

13 $\frac{1}{24} = 0.041\dot{6}$ **14** $\frac{3}{24} = 0.125$

15 $\frac{12}{24} = 0.5$ **16** $\frac{4}{24} = 0.1\dot{6}$

17

	1	2	3	4
H	H 1	H 2	H 3	H 4
T	T 1	T 2	T 3	T 4

18 $\frac{1}{8} = 0.125$ **19** $\frac{4}{8} = 0.5$

20 0 **21** $\frac{5}{8} = 0.625$

2 Long run probability (pp. 12–13)

1 P(bus) = 0.7
P(walked) = $0.22\dot{7}$
P(driven) = $0.07\dot{2}$

2 P(Excellence) = 0.25
P(Merit) = 0.4643
P(Achieved) = 0.2143
P(Not Achieved) = 0.0714

3 **a** 0.225 **b** 0.55 **c** 40.63%
4 **a** 0.0813 **b** 0.4563 **c** 91.88%
5 **a** 39 **b** 0.325 **c** 0.65

Expected number of outcomes (p. 14)

1 40 heads **2** 30 times
3 79 or 80 people **4** 400 boys
5 1 or 2 eggs **6** 10 or 11 hands

Combining probabilities — probability trees (pp. 15–21)

1 **a**

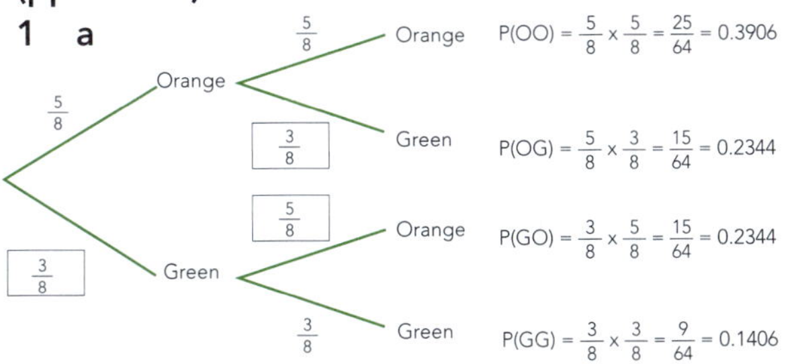

b $\frac{25}{64}$ or 0.3906 **c** $\frac{30}{64}$ or 0.4688

d $\frac{34}{64}$ or 0.5313 **e** $\frac{9}{64}$ or 0.1406

f $\frac{39}{64}$ or 0.6094 **g** $\frac{25}{64}$ x 200 = 78 times

h $\frac{39}{64}$ x 200 = 122 times

2 **a**

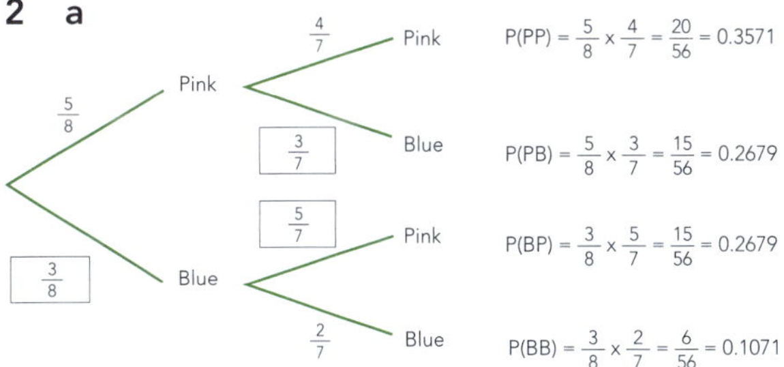

b $\frac{20}{56}$ or 0.3571 **c** $\frac{30}{56}$ or 0.5358

d $\frac{26}{56}$ or 0.4643 **e** $\frac{6}{56}$ or 0.1071

f $\frac{36}{56}$ or 0.6429 **g** 71

h 129

3 **a**

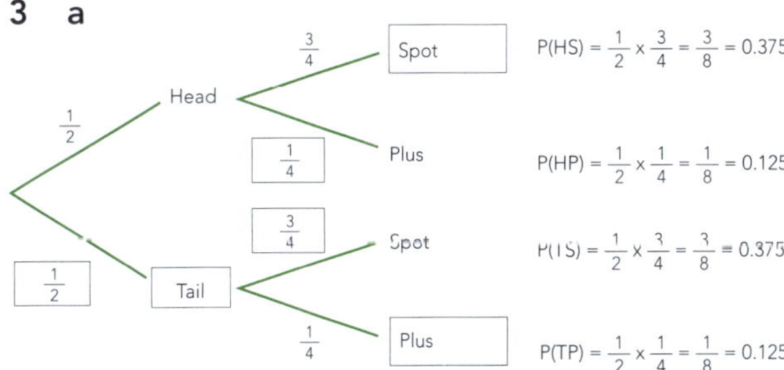

b $\frac{4}{8}$ or 0.5 **c** $\frac{1}{8}$ or 0.125

d $\frac{3}{8}$ or 0.375 **e** $\frac{7}{8}$ or 0.875

f $\frac{5}{8}$ or 0.625 **g** $\frac{3}{8}$ or 0.375

h $\frac{1}{8}$ or 0.125

4 **a**

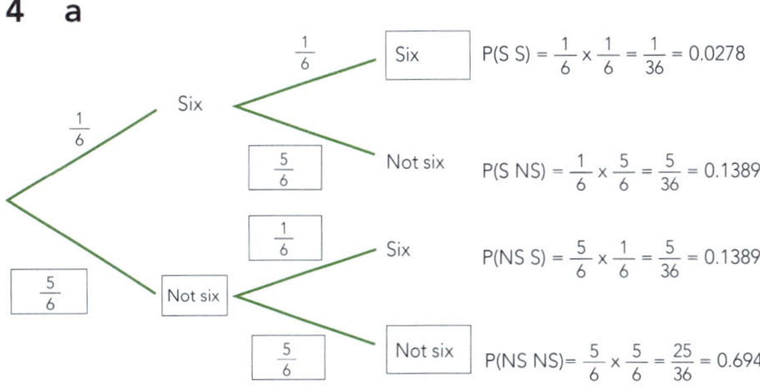

b $\frac{1}{6} = 0.1\dot{6}$ c $\frac{5}{36}$ or 0.1389

d $\frac{11}{36}$ or 0.3056 e $\frac{25}{36}$ or 0.6944

f They add to one because you must either get a six or not get a six in the first two throws.

g 24

h $\frac{25}{36} \times \frac{1}{6} = \frac{25}{216}$ or 0.1157

5 a $\frac{1}{4}$ or 0.25 b $\frac{1}{2}$ or 0.5

c 75% d 25

6 a $\frac{24}{100}$ or 0.24 b 62%

c 247 d 115

Mixing it up (pp. 22–23)

1 a 1 b $\frac{5}{8}$ or 0.625

c $\frac{7}{8}$ or 0.875 d 0.875 x 80 = 70

e $\frac{1}{4}$ or 0.25 f $\frac{1}{4}$ or 0.25

g

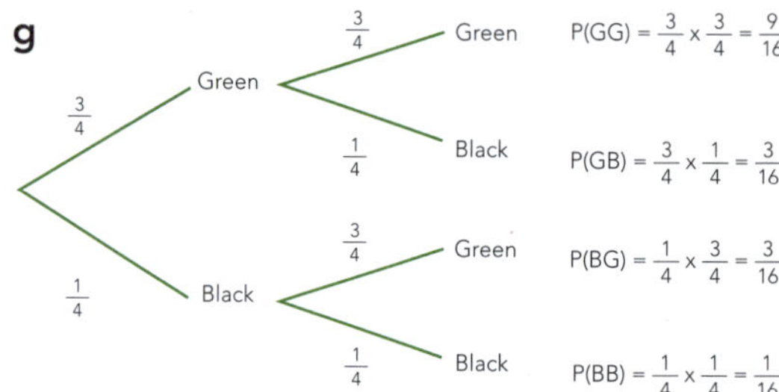

i $\frac{3}{16} = 0.1875$ ii $\frac{6}{16} = 0.375$

iii $\frac{9}{16} \times 80 = 45$

2 a $\frac{1}{6}$ or $\frac{6}{36}$ or $0.1\dot{6}$ b $\frac{4}{36} = 0.\dot{1}$

Turns to finish	one	two	more than two
Probability	$\frac{6}{36}$	$\frac{4}{36}$	$\frac{26}{36}$

c $\frac{26}{36}$ or $0.7\dot{2}$ d 0.65

e The probability from her experiment is lower than the calculated probability. She did only 60 trials, so she might just have been lucky.

f I would expect that the probability from her experiment would be close to $0.7\dot{2}$.

Probability investigations (pp. 24–41)

Note: If your answers are different, check them with your teacher.

1 Planning an investigation (pp. 24–29)

a Questions, trials, outcomes and events (pp. 24–25)

Question	One trial	Outcomes	Event
If I roll two dice and add their numbers, what is the probability that they add to 10 or more?	Rolling two dice.	• Getting dice that add to 2, 3, 4, 5, 6, 7, 8 or 9. • Getting dice that add to 10, 11 or 12.	• Getting dice that add to 10, 11 or 12.
If I have five shots at getting a netball through the hoop from just inside the circle, what is the probability that I get fewer than three through the hoop?	Having five attempts to get a netball through the hoop.	• Getting 0, 1 or 2 goals. • Getting 3 or 4 goals.	• Getting 0, 1 or 2 goals.
I have a bag containing 10 lollies: 4 red, 3 green, 2 yellow and 1 blue. If I pick two lollies together, what is the probability that they are different colours?	Picking two lollies together.	• Picking lollies that are the same colour. • Picking lollies that are different colours.	• Picking lollies that are different colours.
I have a bag containing 10 lollies: 4 red, 3 green, 2 yellow and 1 blue. If I pick lollies one at a time without replacement, what is the probability that I have to pick four or more lollies before I get a red one?	Picking lollies until a red one appears.	• Picking 1, 2 or 3 lollies before getting a red one. • Picking 4 or more lollies before getting a red one.	• Picking 4 or more lollies before getting a red one.
When tossing a coin three times, what is the probability of getting no heads?	Tossing a coin three times.	• Getting 0 heads. • Getting 1, 2 or 3 heads.	• Getting 0 heads.
When tossing a coin, a run occurs when two or more heads or tails occur in a row. If I toss a coin until I have one completed run, what is the probability that a run is more than three heads or tails long?	Tossing a coin until I get a completed run.	• Getting a run of 2 or 3. • Getting a run of 4 or more.	• Getting a run of 4 or more.

ISBN: 9780170416023

b List the steps needed to carry out your investigation and describe how you will record your results (pp. 26–27)

Question	Description of steps and recording of results
If I roll two dice and add their numbers, what is the probability that they add to 10 or more?	I will put two dice in a cup shake them, and then tip them from a height of about 20 cm onto a table top. I will add the two numbers together and write down the total.
If I have five shots at getting a netball through the hoop from just inside the circle, what is the probability that I get fewer than three through the hoop?	I will find five netballs. I will attempt to shoot each through the hoop from the same spot, just inside the circle. I will write down the number that go through the hoop from each set of five. I will do this 10 times, and then take a break or do more the following day.
I have a bag containing 10 lollies: 4 red, 3 green, 2 yellow and 1 blue. If I pick two lollies together, what is the probability that they are different colours?	I will place the lollies which are identical apart from their colour in a bag which I can't see through. I will shake the lollies and put my hand in and pick out two. I will write down their colours, and replace them in the bag.
I have a bag containing 10 lollies: 4 red, 3 green, 2 yellow and 1 blue. If I pick lollies one at a time without replacement, what is the probability that I have to pick four or more lollies before I get a red one?	I will place the lollies which are identical apart from their colour in a bag which I can't see through. I will shake the lollies. I will pick out lollies one at a time, putting each on the table and leaving them there until I get a red one. When a red lolly appears, I will count how many I have on the table, write down the number and then replace the lollies in the bag.
When tossing a coin three times, what is the probability of getting no heads?	I will toss a coin three times, then count and write down the number of heads.
When tossing a coin, a run occurs when two or more heads or tails occur in a row. If I toss a coin until I have one completed run, what is the probability that a run is more than three heads or tails long?	I will toss a coin and record whether a head or tail appears. I keep tossing the coin until I have got a completed run. I count and write down the number of times two, three, four or more heads or tails occur consecutively.

c Number of trials and prediction (pp. 28–29)

Question	Number of trials	Prediction
If I roll two dice and add their numbers, what is the probability that they add to 10 or more?	I will do 80 trials because this will be quite quick to do, and I think 80 trials should give me a good estimate of the probability.	I don't think this will happen very often because I would have to get two fives, a five and a six or two sixes. I think the probability will be about 0.1 or 0.2.
If I have five shots at getting a netball through the hoop from just inside the circle, what is the probability that I get fewer than three through the hoop?	I will do only 50 trials because performing each trial will take quite a lot of time, and my arm and shoulder will get tired. I think 50 trials should give me a reasonable estimate of the probability.	I have done a lot of practice at shooting goals, so I think that I will get fewer than three through the hoop about a third of the time, so I think the probability will probably be about 0.3.
I have a bag containing 10 lollies: 4 red, 3 green, 2 yellow and 1 blue. If I pick two lollies together, what is the probability that they are different colours?	I will do 80 trials because this will be quite quick to do, and I think 80 trials should give me a good estimate of the probability.	I think that I will pick out lollies with different colours more than half of the time, so my estimate for the probability is about 0.6 or 0.7.
I have a bag containing 10 lollies: 4 red, 3 green, 2 yellow and 1 blue. If I pick lollies one at a time without replacement, what is the probability that I have to pick four or more lollies before I get a red one?	I will do 80 trials because this will be quite quick to do, and I think 80 trials should give me a good estimate of the probability.	I think I will mostly pick out a red lolly in the first three I select, so my estimate for the probability is about 0.2.
When tossing a coin three times, what is the probability of getting no heads?	I will do 80 trials because this will be quite quick to do, and I think 80 trials should give me a good estimate of the probability.	I think that it is not very likely that I will get no heads from three coin tosses, so my estimate is that the probability is about 0.1.
When tossing a coin, a run occurs when two or more heads or tails occur in a row. If I toss a coin until I have one completed run, what is the probability that a run is more than three heads or tails long?	I will do 60 trials because it might take quite a long time before I get 60 runs of two or more.	I think most of the runs will be two long, and runs of three will not happen very often. My estimate is that the probability will be about 0.2.

2 Recording and displaying results (pp. 30–37)

1 a

Sum	Tally	Frequency	Probability	
2	II	2	$\frac{2}{80}$	0.025
3	IIII	4	$\frac{4}{80}$	0.05
4	卌 II	7	$\frac{7}{80}$	0.0875
5	卌 IIII	9	$\frac{9}{80}$	0.1125
6	卌 卌 II	12	$\frac{12}{80}$	0.15
7	卌 卌	10	$\frac{10}{80}$	0.125
8	卌 卌 III	13	$\frac{13}{80}$	0.1625
9	卌 IIII	9	$\frac{9}{80}$	0.1125
10	卌 IIII	9	$\frac{9}{80}$	0.1125
11	II	2	$\frac{2}{80}$	0.025
12	III	3	$\frac{3}{80}$	0.0375
Total		**80**	**1**	**1**

b

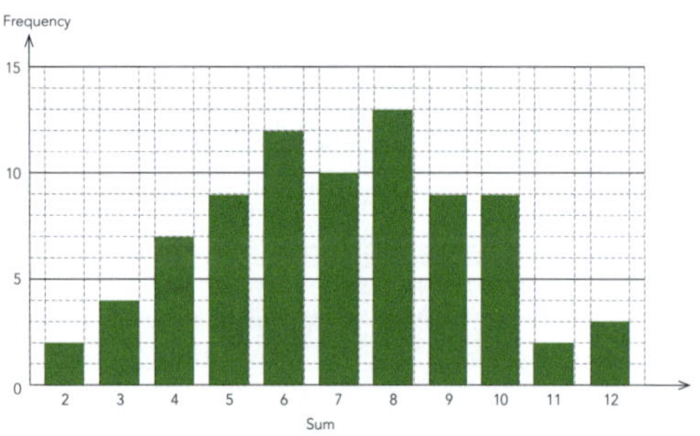

c

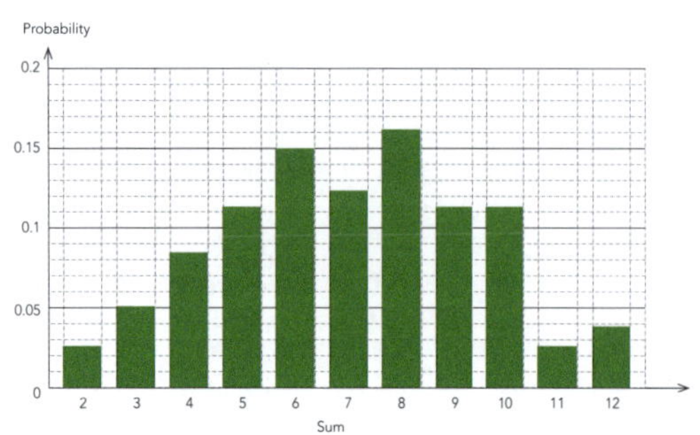

d **Experimental probability** that the sum was 10 or more

= P(10) + P(11) + P(12)

= 0.1125 + 0.025 + 0.0375

= 0.175

2 a

					Totals for each row
GGNNG	GNGGN	NGNNG	GGGNG	NGGGG	**33244**
NGGGN	NNNGN	NGNNG	GNNGN	GGNGN	**31223**
NNGGN	GNGNN	GGGGN	GNGGN	GNGGG	**22434**
GGNNG	NNNGN	GNNGG	GGNNG	GNGNG	**31333**
GGNNN	GGNNG	NNGNG	GNNGN	GNGNN	**23222**
GNNNN	NGNNG	NGNNN	GNGNG	GNGNN	**12132**
NNGGG	GGNNN	GNNGG	GGGGG	NNGGN	**32352**
NGGGN	GGNGN	NGNNN	GGNGG	GNGGG	**33144**
NGGGG	GGNGN	GNGNG	GNNGN	NGGGG	**43324**
GNNNG	NNGGN	NNGGG	NGGNN	GNNNG	**22422**

b

Number of goals	Tally	Frequency	Probability	
0		0	$\frac{0}{50}$	0
1	卌	5	$\frac{5}{50}$	0.1
2	卌 卌 卌 III	18	$\frac{18}{50}$	0.36
3	卌 卌 卌 II	17	$\frac{17}{50}$	0.34
4	卌 IIII	9	$\frac{9}{50}$	0.18
5	I	1	$\frac{1}{50}$	0.02
Total		**50**	**1**	**1**

ISBN: 9780170416023

c

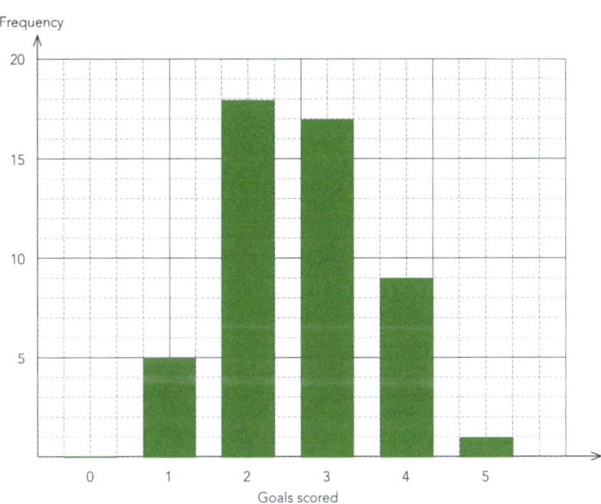

d

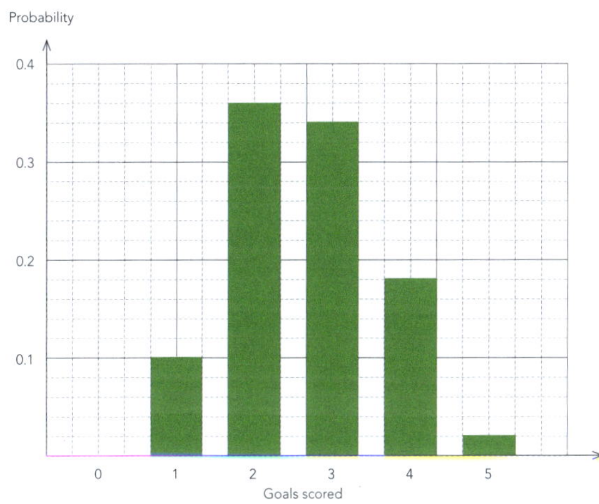

e **Experimental probability**

= P(0) + P(1) + P(2)

= 0 + 0.1 + 0.36

= 0.46

3 Identifying patterns and discussing the data (pp. 38–39)

1
- I was most likely to get sums of 6, 7 or 8.
- I was least likely to get 2, 11 or 12.
- If I had got a few more 11s and 7s, the distribution would have been approximately bell-shaped.

2
- I was most likely to get 2 or 3 goals out of a possible five.
- I was least likely to get 0, 1 or 5 goals.
- I always got at least one goal, although if I did more trials it is possible I may have got no goals from five shots.

4 Writing a conclusion (pp. 40–41)

1 The experimental probability that the dice add to 10 or more is 0.175. My prediction for the probability was 0.1 or 0.2. This was about the same as the experimental probability. My experimental probability seems reasonable because the probability of getting 10 or more must be quite low. Possible sources of error are that one or both of the dice is not a fair die, and that I didn't add the totals correctly. I don't think either of these is very likely. I think my estimate for the probability is fairly reliable because I did 80 trials. I could improve its reliability by doing more trials.

2 The experimental probability that I get fewer than three balls through the hoop is 0.46. My prediction for the probability was 0.3. This was quite a lot less than the experimental probability. My experimental probability seems surprising because I didn't think I was very good at shooting goals. Possible sources of error are that I may have not stood in quite the same spot for all attempts, and my shooting may have improved throughout the experiment. I think my estimate for the probability is fairly reliable because I did 60 trials. I could improve its reliability by doing more trials.

Optional extras (pp. 42–57)

1 Plotting probabilities throughout an experiment (pp. 42–53)

1 a

List of sums	Total number of trials	Total number of trials where sum is ≥ 10	P(sum is ≥ 10)	
6 5 6 8 7	5	0	$\frac{0}{5}$	0
5 3 10 6 5	10	1	$\frac{1}{10}$	0.1
8 7 8 4 5	15	1	$\frac{1}{15}$	$0.0\dot{6}$
8 7 9 8 9	20	1	$\frac{1}{20}$	0.05
7 11 10 6 9	25	3	$\frac{3}{25}$	0.12
6 10 2 8 8	30	4	$\frac{4}{30}$	$0.1\dot{3}$
10 10 12 4 9	35	7	$\frac{7}{35}$	0.2

ISBN: 9780170416023

List of sums	Total number of trials	Total number of trials where sum is ≥ 10	P(sum is ≥ 10)	
6 10 4 7 8	40	8	$\frac{8}{40}$	0.2
4 6 12 9 8	45	9	$\frac{9}{45}$	0.2
6 4 11 6 4	50	10	$\frac{10}{50}$	0.2
9 6 4 5 2	55	10	$\frac{10}{55}$	$0.\dot{1}\dot{8}$
7 10 8 9 6	60	11	$\frac{11}{60}$	$0.18\dot{3}$
10 7 7 10 5	65	13	$\frac{13}{65}$	0.2
9 7 6 8 5	70	13	$\frac{13}{70}$	0.1857
8 9 3 5 3	75	13	$\frac{13}{75}$	$0.17\dot{3}$
12 7 8 3 5	80	14	$\frac{14}{80}$	0.175

b

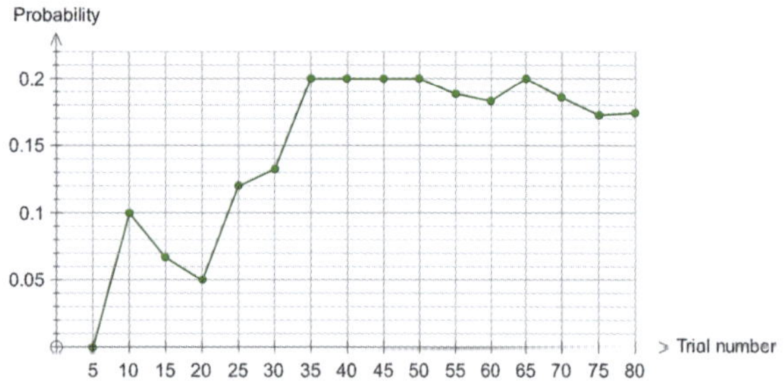

c There is a lot of variation at the start, but from 35 trials onwards the probabilities are fairly stable between 0.17 and 0.2.

d The probability of getting 10 or more when two dice are thrown is about 0.18.

e I can be reasonably certain that it is about 0.18 because I did 80 trials.

f In order to get a better estimate of the probability I would need to do more trials — at least 100.

2 a

Number of goals	Total number of trials	Total number of trials with 0, 1 or 2 goals	P(0, 1 or 2 goals)	
33244	5	1	$\frac{1}{5}$	0.2
31223	10	4	$\frac{4}{10}$	0.4
22434	15	6	$\frac{6}{15}$	0.4
31333	20	7	$\frac{7}{20}$	0.35
23222	25	11	$\frac{11}{25}$	0.44
12132	30	15	$\frac{15}{30}$	0.5
32352	35	17	$\frac{17}{35}$	0.4857
33144	40	18	$\frac{18}{40}$	0.45
43324	45	19	$\frac{19}{45}$	$0.4\dot{2}$
22322	50	23	$\frac{23}{50}$	0.46

b

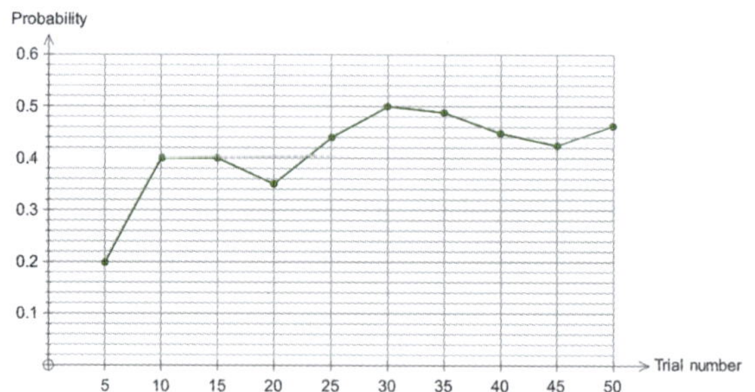

c
- The probability that I get fewer than three balls through the hoop is variable over the first 20 trials.
- From 25 trials onwards it becomes more stable, between 0.42 and 0.5.
- I think that the probability is about 0.46.
- For a more reliable estimate, I would need to do more trials.

ISBN: 9780170416023

3 a

Total number of drawing pins dropped	Number in each trial landing with point up	Total number that have landed point up	P(sum is ≥ 10)	
10	5	5	$\frac{5}{10}$	0.5
20	6	11	$\frac{11}{20}$	0.55
30	6	17	$\frac{17}{30}$	$0.5\dot{6}$
40	7	24	$\frac{24}{40}$	0.6
50	5	29	$\frac{29}{50}$	0.58
60	4	33	$\frac{33}{60}$	0.55
70	4	37	$\frac{37}{70}$	0.5286
80	6	43	$\frac{43}{80}$	0.5375
90	8	51	$\frac{51}{90}$	$0.5\dot{6}$
100	5	56	$\frac{56}{100}$	0.56
110	8	64	$\frac{64}{110}$	$0.5\dot{8}\dot{1}$
120	10	74	$\frac{74}{120}$	$0.61\dot{6}$
130	4	78	$\frac{78}{130}$	0.6
140	7	85	$\frac{85}{140}$	0.6071
150	6	91	$\frac{91}{150}$	$0.60\dot{6}$

b

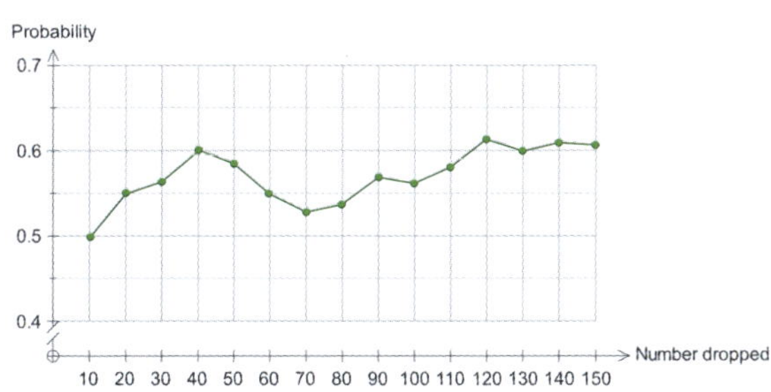

c

- There is much more variation in the probabilities that a drawing pin lands point up for the first 100 trials.
- For the last 30 trials the probability stabilises at about 0.6.
- I think the probability that a drawing pin lands point up is about 0.6.
- I would need to do more trials to find a more reliable probability.

4 a

Trial number	Result	Total 'down'	P('down')	
1	down	1	$\frac{1}{1}$	1.0
2	up	1	$\frac{1}{2}$	0.5
3	down	2	$\frac{2}{3}$	$0.\dot{6}$
4	down	3	$\frac{3}{4}$	0.75
5	up	3	$\frac{3}{5}$	0.6
6	down	4	$\frac{4}{6}$	$0.\dot{6}$
7	up	4	$\frac{4}{7}$	0.5714
8	up	4	$\frac{4}{8}$	0.5
9	up	4	$\frac{4}{9}$	$0.\dot{4}$
10	down	5	$\frac{5}{10}$	0.5
11	down	6	$\frac{6}{11}$	$0.5\dot{4}$
12	down	7	$\frac{7}{12}$	$0.58\dot{3}$
13	up	7	$\frac{7}{13}$	0.5385
14	down	8	$\frac{8}{14}$	05714
15	up	8	$\frac{8}{15}$	$0.5\dot{3}$
16	down	9	$\frac{9}{16}$	0.5625
17	down	10	$\frac{10}{17}$	0.5882
18	up	10	$\frac{10}{18}$	$0.\dot{5}$
19	down	11	$\frac{11}{19}$	0.5789
20	down	12	$\frac{12}{20}$	0.6

ISBN: 9780170416023

b

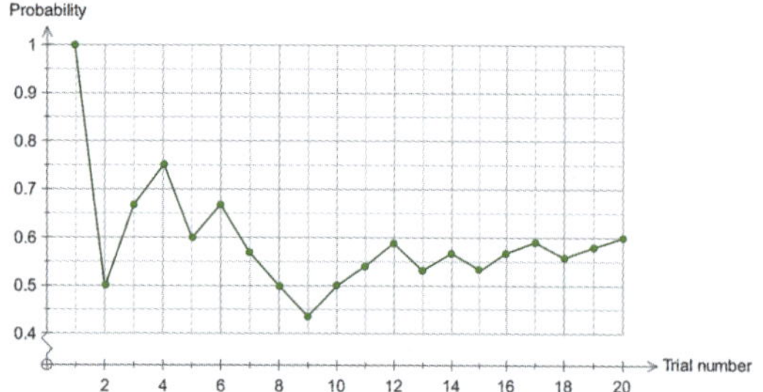

c
- There is a lot of variation in the probabilities that toast lands jam side down for the first 12 drops.
- After that the graph stabilises so that it is mostly between 0.5 and 0.6.
- I think the probability that toast lands jam side down is probably between 0.55 and 0.6, but only 20 trials were done.
- Ngaire should do a lot more trials in order to get a more reliable estimate.

2 Calculating the theoretical probability (pp. 54–57)

1 Calculation of the theoretical probability:
Because the probability of getting each number on a fair die is equally likely, I can draw a table showing all the possible combinations:

	1	2	3	4	5	6
1	1 1	1 2	1 3	1 4	1 5	1 6
2	2 1	2 2	2 3	2 4	2 5	2 6
3	3 1	3 2	3 3	3 4	3 5	3 6
4	4 1	4 2	4 3	4 4	4 5	4 6
5	5 1	5 2	5 3	5 4	5 5	5 6
6	6 1	6 2	6 3	6 4	6 5	6 6

The six combinations which add to 10 or more are shown in bold. Because there are 36 possibilities, the theoretical probability of 10 or more

$= \frac{6}{36} = 0.1\dot{6}$.

Comparison with the experimental probability, and discussion:
The experimental probability was 0.175 which is close to $0.1\dot{6}$. This is probably because I did 80 trials. However, I would expect the experimental probability would have been even closer to $0.1\dot{6}$ if I had done more trials.

2 Calculation of the theoretical probability:

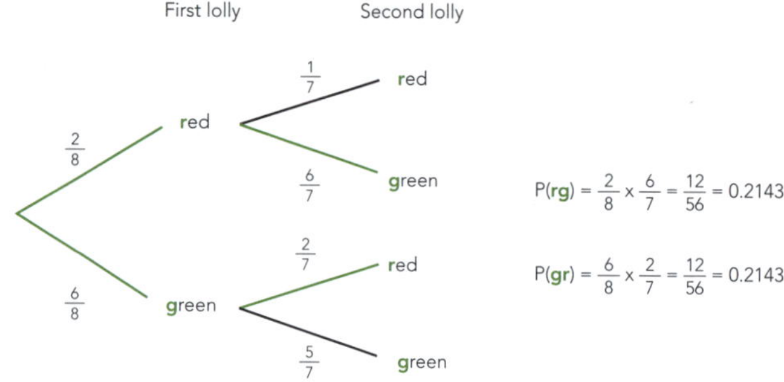

$\therefore$ P(rg or gr) = 2 x 0.2143 = 0.4286

Comparison with the experimental probability, and discussion:
The experimental probability was 0.39 which is a little lower than the theoretical probability. Only 60 trials were done. I would expect that the experimental probability would be closer to the theoretical probability if more trials were done.

3 Calculation of the theoretical probability:
There are 12 equally likely outcomes:

	1	2	3	4	5	6
H	H 1	H 2	H 3	H 4	H 5	H 6
T	T 1	T 2	T 3	T 4	T 5	T 6

Each has the probability of $\frac{1}{12}$, so the probability of H5 or H6 = $\frac{2}{12} = 0.1\dot{6}$.

Comparison with the experimental probability, and discussion:
The experimental probability was 0.19, which is close to $0.1\dot{6}$, but a more reliable estimate could be obtained by doing more trials.

4 Calculation of the theoretical probability:

P(red or blue pencil) = $\frac{4}{6}$

P(yellow pencil) = $\frac{2}{6}$

P(red or blue pencil followed by a yellow pencil) = $\frac{4}{6} \times \frac{2}{6} = 0.\dot{2}$.

Comparison with the experimental probability, and discussion:
The experimental probability was higher than the theoretical probability. However, Jamie did only 50 trials, so she could improve her estimate by doing more trials.

ISBN: 9780170416023

Practice tasks (pp. 62–75)

Practice task one (pp. 62–66)

Card game

Plan of investigation

Question: Six cards, four with turtles and two with ruru, are turned face down. When two cards are drawn without replacement, what is the probability of getting exactly one ruru (or one of each type of card)?

Outcomes: 1 Drawing exactly one ruru.
2 Drawing no ruru or two ruru.

Event of interest: Drawing exactly one ruru.

List of the steps she could have used to carry out the investigation:

1. She turned all the cards face down.
2. She drew out one card, and without replacing it, then she drew a second.
3. She then mixed up the cards and repeated the process.

Explanation of how her results might have been recorded: She made a table and wrote down the number of ruru for each trial.

Number of trials/observations: She did 60 trials.

You make a prediction: I think that the probability that she picked up exactly one ruru card is about a half. Two out of the six cards have ruru, so it seems quite likely that she will get exactly one.

Record, display and analysis of results

Table showing results, frequencies and probabilities:

Number of ruru	Total number of trials	Total number with exactly one of each design	P(one of each)	
02010	5	1	$\frac{1}{5}$	0.2
11101	10	5	$\frac{5}{10}$	0.5
00111	15	8	$\frac{8}{15}$	$0.5\dot{3}$
10011	20	11	$\frac{11}{20}$	0.55
10110	25	14	$\frac{14}{25}$	0.56
01110	30	17	$\frac{17}{30}$	$0.5\dot{6}$
12100	35	19	$\frac{19}{35}$	0.5429
01001	40	21	$\frac{21}{40}$	0.525
00111	45	24	$\frac{24}{45}$	$0.5\dot{3}$
01211	50	27	$\frac{27}{50}$	0.54
11101	55	31	$\frac{31}{55}$	0.5636
21001	60	33	$\frac{33}{60}$	0.55

Frequency graph:

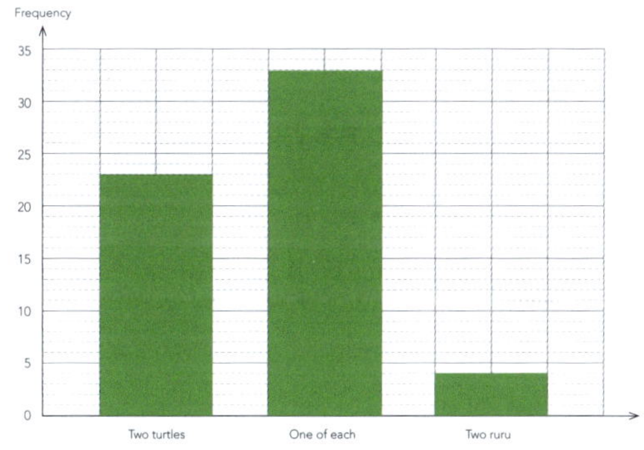

Probability graph:

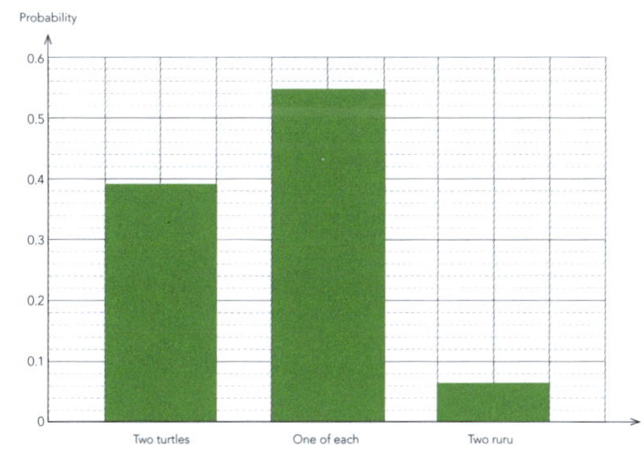

Calculation of experimental probability:

P(exactly one ruru) = $\frac{33}{60}$ = 0.55.

ISBN: 9780170416023

Identify patterns and discuss the data
Huia was most likely to get one of each card type (0.55). She was a bit less likely to get two turtles (about 0.4), and she was very unlikely to get two ruru.

Conclusion
Answer to the question: The experimental probability that she picked up exactly one ruru is 0.55.

Comparison with prediction: This is quite close to my prediction that the probability would be about a half.

Does the experimental probability seem reasonable? I think the experimental probability seems reasonable because it was quite close to what I predicted.

Possible sources of error: I have assumed she made the backs of all the cards identical, that she mixed them thoroughly after each trial and she recorded the data accurately. If she did all of these, there should be no sources of error.

Comment on the reliability of the estimate for the probability, and suggestions for how it could be improved: I think the reliability of the estimate is reasonable, but it could be improved by doing more trials.

Optional extras:
1 Plot of the probabilities throughout the experiment
Calculation of the experimental probabilities: Done in table above.

Line graph of probabilities

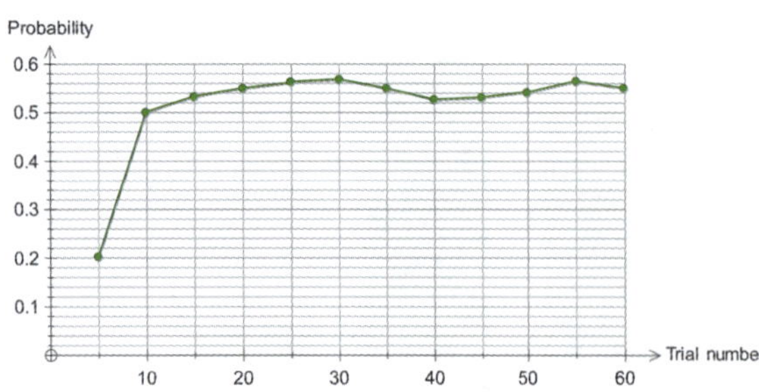

Discussion: There is a big jump in the probabilities between the fifth and the tenth trials, but after that the probabilities remain very stable; after the fifteenth trial, all are between 0.52 and 0.57. This gives me greater confidence that my experimental probability is reasonable accurate.

2 Calculation of the theoretical probability
Calculations:

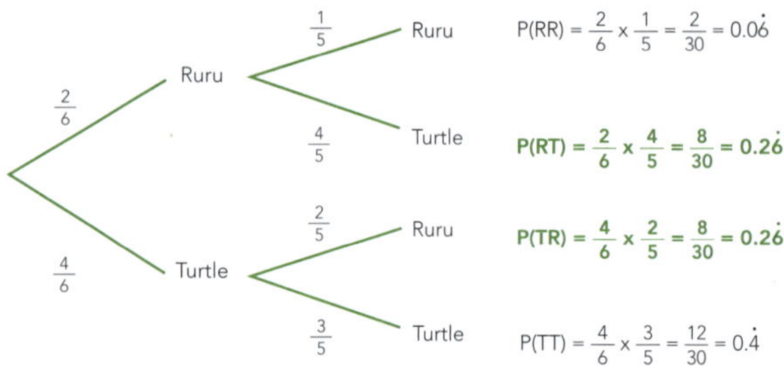

P(exactly one ruru) = $2 \times 0.2\dot{6} = 0.5\dot{3}$.
Comparison with the experimental probability and discussion: The theoretical probability ($0.5\dot{3}$) is a little lower than the experimental probability (0.55). I notice that after 45 trials the experimental probability was exactly the same as the theoretical probability, but between trials 43 and 53, nine out of the eleven trials resulted in exactly one ruru. This was an unusual run, which would explain why my experimental probability was a little high. Doing more trials would almost certainly improve my estimate.

Practice task two (pp. 67–71)

Paper planes
Plan of investigation
Tane will have three throws of his paper plane. What is the probability that in all three throws the plane travels at least 5 metres before hitting the ground? There are two outcomes: All three paper planes travel at least 5 metres or fewer than three planes travel at least 5 metres. The event he was interest in was that all three planes travel at least 5 metres.

Tane needed to:
- mark a line that was exactly 5 metres from the point at which he threw the plane
- throw the plane three times
- for each set of three throws, write down in a table the number that travelled at least 5 metres before hitting the ground.

He did 50 trials.

He estimated that the probability of getting all three planes to travel more than 5 metres would be at least 0.5.

  ISBN: 9780170416023

Record, display and analysis of results

Table showing results, frequencies and probabilities:

Number over 5 m	Total number of trials	Total number where all three flew 5 m	P(all three flew 5 m)	
22313	5	2	$\frac{2}{5}$	0.4
11233	10	4	$\frac{4}{10}$	0.4
21032	15	5	$\frac{5}{15}$	$0.3\dot{3}$
13211	20	6	$\frac{6}{20}$	0.3
23301	25	8	$\frac{8}{25}$	0.32
02321	30	9	$\frac{9}{30}$	0.3
33221	35	11	$\frac{11}{35}$	0.3143
30121	40	12	$\frac{12}{40}$	0.3
32022	45	13	$\frac{13}{45}$	$0.2\dot{8}$
22321	50	14	$\frac{14}{50}$	0.28

Frequency graph:

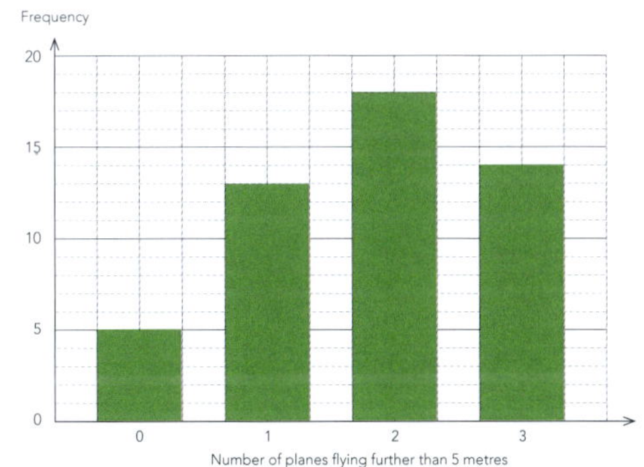

Probability graph:

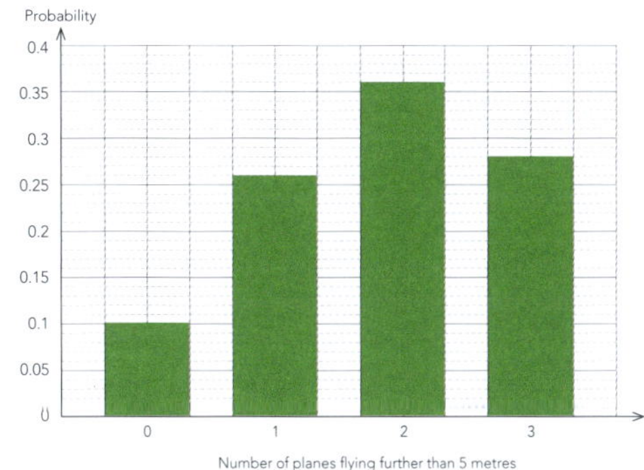

Calculation of experimental probability:

P(three planes travel further than 5 m)

$$= \frac{14}{50} = 0.28.$$

Identify patterns and discuss the data

The probability that in two of Tane's three throws the plane travelled at least 5 metres before hitting the ground was highest. It was less likely that all three travelled at least 5 metres, and even less likely that only one travelled 5 metres. Least likely of all was that none of his throws resulted in the plane staying in the air for 5 metres.

Conclusion

- The experimental probability that in all three throws the plane travels at least 5 metres before hitting the ground was 0.28.
- This is much lower than Tane predicted: he estimated that the probability of getting all three planes to travel more than 5 metres would be at least 0.5.
- This means that his design is not nearly as good as he thought it was, so he should consider changing it.
- He did only 50 trials. It is possible that if he did more, he might find that the probability was a little higher, but almost certainly it would not be close to 0.5.
- I have assumed that his plane remained in good condition, but it is likely that in 150 throws, it became a bit beaten up. I have assumed that any replacement plane that he made was identical to the original one.

ISBN: 9780170416023

Optional extra: Plot of the probabilities throughout the experiment

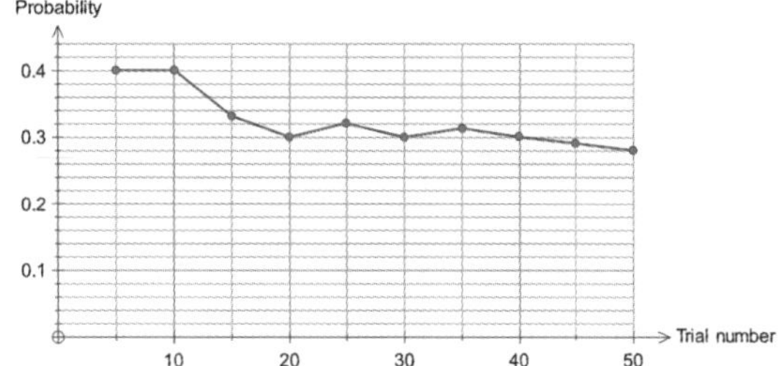

- The probabilities were more variable at the start, dropping a lot between the tenth and the twentieth throw.
- Towards the end, the probabilities were more stable, but they were dropping steadily over the final 15 trials to 0.28. This means that it is very unlikely that if Tane did more trials, the probability would increase to anything close to his estimate of 0.5.

Practice task three (pp. 72–75)

Bottle flip
Ask your teacher to check your report.

ISBN: 9780170416023